The Work of Donald Meltzer Revisited

'This is a deeply inspiring book on the extraordinary contributions of Donald Meltzer to psychoanalysis. From all the authors we hear of Meltzer's surpassing originality, his wit and humor and the presence of his 'clinical intuition' they experienced in working and being in supervision with him. This book provides a unique set of perspectives on his work and influence and how his thinking is being used in different fields. It will give pleasure and much food for thought to readers interested in the state of psychoanalysis.'

Angelika Staehle, *Training and Supervising Analyst for Adults, Adolescents and Children German Psychoanalytic Association (DPV), former chair and current consultant of the Psychoanalytic Education Committee IPA*

'Meltzer's deep conviction in the unconscious workings of the mind is at the foundation of all his work, imbuing psychoanalytic practice with awe, mystery, surprise, boldness, and a profound sense of intimacy. The admirable writers in this volume each highlight a different facet of Meltzer's prolific work, illustrating, with rich clinical material, how these notions come alive in our consulting rooms. It is an invaluable contribution to our struggle to grasp the enigma of the psychoanalytic encounter.'

Avner Bergstein, *Israel Psychoanalytic Society, author of* Bion and Meltzer's Expeditions into Unmapped Mental Life: Beyond the Spectrum in Psychoanalysis

The Work of Donald Meltzer Revisited: 100 Years After His Birth returns to and reassesses the contributions of Donald Meltzer, one of the most significant disciples of Melanie Klein and who was deeply inspired by Wilfred Bion.

An international selection of leading contributors delves into the work of Meltzer and explores a wide range of topics introduced and developed by him, including the claustrum, adhesive identification and preformed and analytic transference. The book also considers Meltzer's approach to dreams and presents relevant clinical vignettes. It provides a thorough account of the way Meltzer's contributions have evolved and enriched psychoanalytic theory and practice.

The Work of Donald Meltzer Revisited: 100 Years After His Birth will be of great interest to students and psychoanalysts both in practice and in training, especially those less familiar with the legacy of Meltzer's work.

Carlos Moguillansky is MD, Master in Culture, Training and Supervising Analyst at the Buenos Aires Psychoanalytical Association and former Scientific Secretary and President of APDEBA. He is a former member of the board of *The International Journal of Psychoanalysis* and a current member of the IPA Publications Committee.

Gabriela Legorreta, PhD, is a member of the Montreal Psychoanalytic Society (French section of the Canadian Psychoanalytic Society), as well as a Training and Supervising Analyst at the Montreal Psychoanalytic Institute and President Elect of the Canadian Psychoanalytic Society. She is former Chair and present Consultant of the IPA Publications Committee.

The International Psychoanalytical Association Psychoanalytic Classics Revisited Series

Series Editor: Silvia Flechner

IPA Publications Committee

Natacha Delgado, Nergis Güleç, Thomas Marcacci, Carlos Moguillansky, Rafael Mondrzak, Angela M. Vuotto, Gabriela Legoretta (consultant)

Titles in this series

Playing and Reality Revisited: A New Look at Winnicott's Classic Work
Edited by Gennaro Saragnano and Christian Seulin

Attacks on Linking Revisited: A New Look at Bion's Classic Work
Catalina Bronstein

André Green Revisited: Representation and the Work of the Negative
Edited by Gail S. Reed and Howard B. Levine

Psychoanalysis of the Psychoanalytic Frame Revisited: A New Look at José Bleger's Classic Work
Edited by Carlos Moguillansky and Howard B. Levine

The Work of Donald Meltzer Revisited: 100 Years After His Birth
Edited by Carlos Moguillansky and Gabriela Legorreta

The Work of Donald Meltzer Revisited

Revisited

100 Years After His Birth

**Edited by Carlos Moguillansky
and Gabriela Legorreta**

Routledge
Taylor & Francis Group

LONDON AND NEW YORK

Designed cover image: © kwasny221 / Getty Images

First published 2024
by Routledge
4 Park Square, Milton Park, Abingdon, Oxon OX14 4RN

and by Routledge
605 Third Avenue, New York, NY 10158

Routledge is an imprint of the Taylor & Francis Group, an informal business

British Library Cataloguing-in-Publication Data
A catalogue record for this book is available from the British Library

ISBN: 978-1-032-57971-9 (hbk)
ISBN: 978-1-032-57970-2 (pbk)
ISBN: 978-1-003-44186-1 (ebk)

DOI: 10.4324/9781003441861

Typeset in Palatino
by codeMantra

Contents

Series Editor's Foreword

Revisiting the Work of Donald Meltzer

Edited by Carlos Moguillansky
and Gabriela Legorreta

The Publications Committee of the IPA is pleased to present the new book *The Work of Donald Meltzer Revisited* edited by Carlos Moguillansky and Gabriela Legorreta. This book is part of the series "Classic Revisited" of the IPA.

The "Classic Revisited" series was launched by Gennaro Saragnano in 2015. Its aim is to make available to psychoanalysts and other scholars in related fields, a reinterpretation of the classics of psychoanalysis by authoritative colleagues from different regions of the IPA, including recent developments in contemporary psychoanalysis.

Donald Meltzer was born in New Jersey (USA) in 1922. After completing his psychiatric training in St. Louis, Missouri, he decided to go into child psychiatry and somehow found his way to London to have an analysis with Melanie Klein. While training in the British Psychoanalytical Society, he supervised his adult cases with Hanna Segal and Herbert Rosenfeld and later his child cases with Betty Joseph, Esther Bick and Hanna Segal. In later years, he especially acknowledged the influence of Esther Bick, Roger Money-Kyrle and Wilfred Bion.

In *Sexual States of Mind* (1973), Meltzer proposed a structural revision of the theory of psychosexual development, perversions and addictions, with an emphasis on the introjective quality of adult sexuality in adolescent states of mind. Chapters on "Tyranny," "The Psychic Reality of Unborn Children" and "On Pornography" also appeared as applications of his theoretical findings.

Explorations in Autism was published in 1975; this book was the result of a cooperative effort with five supervisees and dealt with the fascinating discovery of clinical phenomena in autistic and post-autistic states like dismantling, the impairment of spatial and temporal dimensionality, mindlessness and adhesive identification.

Dreamlife: A Reexamination of the Psychoanalytical Theory and Technique (1984) provides a revised theory of dreaming as unconscious thinking in which meaning is generated. The practice of dream investigation is thoroughly examined. Elena Ortiz wrote the chapter "The language of dreams: On symbolism, aesthetics and interpretation" deepening the subject.

In *Studies in Extended Metapsychology: Clinical Application of Bion's Ideas* (1986), Meltzer considered the importance of the development of emotional states and added clinical congruity to much of Bion's theory, in particular, the interrelation between "Container-Contained," the concept of "Vertices," "Transformation in Hallucinosis" and "Turbulence." His ideas on the claustrum, which he would write extensively in his last book in 1992 were incubated since his anal masturbation paper, get a new airing in these studies.

In *The Apprehension of Beauty* (1988), Meltzer introduces the "aesthetic conflict" as an early phenomenon in the baby's relation to the external world where the aesthetic experience of the budding relationship with the mother stimulates both the wish to know her and the frustration created by the mystery of the unknown aspects of the object. This book, written in cooperation with Meg Harris Williams, also reflects his growing interest in literature, the process of writing and creativity – a subject he had been writing about 25 years earlier in a book called *Painting and the Inner World* (1963) and which appears as a dialogue with the author, the art critic Adrian Stokes. The chapter "Psychoanalysis as a form of art: working with D. Meltzer" written by Meg Harris Williams brings us back to the issue of aesthetic conflict.

The Claustrum: An Investigation of Claustrophobic Phenomena (1992) revisits the concept of projective identification not in terms of quantity or quality of projective mechanisms but in terms of the choice of object that is being projected into. In his thorough phenomenological examination of intrusive identification (as he prefers to call it), Florence Guignard and Ruggero Levy deepen this topic in their chapters.

It is also worth mentioning here a three-volume work published in 1975: *The Kleinian Development* (1975), which was born out of a series of lectures on Freud, Klein and Bion at the Tavistock Clinic, where he exercised a much-appreciated influence in the development of the profession of child psychotherapy, and *A Psychoanalytical Model of the Child-in-the-Family-in-the-Community* (1976) commissioned by the United Nations and co-written with Martha Harris.

Donald Meltzer died in August 2004. His passing deprived psychoanalysis of an innovative thinker and a prolific writer whose pioneering work over the last 50 years influenced a whole generation of colleagues, psychotherapists and mental health workers worldwide. He made an outstanding contribution to understanding the infant's mind; the emotional development of object relations and the psychoanalytical treatment of perversions, narcissistic states and autism. The range and depth of his work, his gift for analyzing the deepest strata of the mind and his sensitivity to primitive modes of functioning made him an outstanding supervisor.

Meltzer was well known internationally as a teacher and supervisor. He favored a workshop-style system for teaching and selecting candidates for psychoanalytic training, outlined in his document "Towards an atelier system." He asked supervisees to submit unedited clinical material sessions rather than the finished papers. Several of his groups and individual supervisees documented their experiences.

Carlos Moguillansky describes about Meltzer that "Their chapters provide a unique spectrum of versions on this subject and introduce a fruitful debate on the nature of emotion and in particular, on the link between emotion and aesthetic experience, both in the apprehension of the beauty of the object and its unique emotional functions and in the pain and the psychic defenses associated with it."

Meltzer states: "There are things that can be learned, but they cannot be taught." Access to the symbolic register requires learning from one's own experience. Virginia Ungar explains this in her chapter: "Tradition is, therefore, a 'handing-down,' a 'delivery.'" In his work, Meltzer often mentions that psychoanalysis can be learned but, paradoxically, cannot be taught. It can thus be said that learning is facilitated and transmitted rather than taught. In his short (but essential) article on the "atelier" system (1971), he described it as an exercise in craftsmanship to be given a place resembling the one represented in the monumental work of Raphael Sanzio, The School of Athens. "This masterpiece depicts a space assembling relaxed looking Master of Philosophy of the like of Socrates, Plato, Aristotle and Parmenides; gods such as Apollo and Minerva; scientists such as Archimedes and others depicted as listening and surely asking questions."

This Committee has the honor of publishing this book edited by the former Chair of the Publications Committee Gabriela Legorreta, and our colleague and friend of the Publications Committee member, Carlos Moguillansky. Both have been important pillars of our committee for many years. We appreciate their efforts to get this book published. This book will be of great value to those who want to deepen in Meltzer's legacy and be inspired by the ideas of our writers.

Silvia Flechner
Series Editor
Chair, IPA Publications Committee

Contributor Biographies

Abbot Bronstein, PhD, is a psychologist and psychoanalyst. He is the editor of the Analyst at Work Section and Associate Editor of *The International Journal of Psychoanalysis*. He is the Co-chair of the Comparative Clinical Methods Working Party in North America (which he introduced and developed) and member and former Training and Supervising Analyst of the San Francisco Center for Psychoanalysis. He was a board member of the International Psychoanalytic Association. He has been a visiting faculty at Emory Psychoanalytic Institute, Oregon Psychoanalytic Institute and has taught and presented widely in North America and Europe. In addition to presenting and publishing numerous papers on the CCM research in North America, he also has written papers on Fetish, Ending analysis, Remote and In-office analysis. He most recently has contributed (co-written with Marie Rudden) a chapter in a Working Party Publication of the IPA. He was honored as the distinguished analyst in 2017 at the meeting of the American Psychoanalytic Association.

Florence Guignard is a Swiss and French psychologist, researcher and psychoanalyst. She is the past Vice-President and Training Analyst of the Paris Society of Psychoanalysis (SPP). She is a Training Member of IPA for Child and Adolescent Psychoanalysis and past Chair and present Counsellor of the IPA Committee On Child and Adolescent Psychoanalysis (COCAP). She founded the Société Européenne pour la Psychanalyse de l'Enfant et de l'Adolescent (SEPEA) in 1994. She was the chair of the team of l'Année Psychanalytique Internationale/IJP 3. She has published more than 300 psychoanalytical papers in Psychoanalytical Reviews and collective books, in French, English, Italian, Spanish, Portuguese, Polish and Turkish. Her books have also been translated to many languages, and they include the following: *Au Vif de l'Infantile* (1996), *Épître à l'objet* (1997), *Quelle Psychanalyse pour le XXIe siècle?* (2015), *Vol. I Concepts psychanalytiques en mouvement, Psychoanalytic concepts and Technique in Development. Psychoanalysis, Neuroscience and Physics* (2020), and *Au Vif de l'Infantile, aujourd'hui* (2020). She has two forthcoming books: *Entretiens avec Florence Guignard. Une autobiographie, avec Sylvie Reignier « Quelle psychanalyse pour le XXIe siècle ? » Volume II : Le psychanalyste dans la cité.*

Meg Harris Williams is a writer and lecturer in literature and psycho-analysis and also a visual artist. She teaches internationally and is a visiting lecturer at the Tavistock Clinic, an honorary member of the Psychoanalytic Center of California and editor of The Harris Meltzer Trust. Her books and papers have been translated into many languages and include the following: *The Apprehension of Beauty* (with Donald Meltzer; 1988), *The Vale of Soulmaking* (2005), *The Aesthetic Development* (2010), *Bion's Dream* (2010), *The Art of Personality in Literature and Psycho-analysis* (2017), *Dream Sequences in Shakespeare* (2021) and *Donald Meltzer: A Contemporary Introduction* (2021).

Cláudio Laks Eizirik is a Training and Supervising Analyst, Porto Alegre Psychoanalytic Society; Professor Emeritus of Psychiatry, Federal University of Rio Grande do Sul; former President of the IPA and FEPAL; Sigourney Award winner of 2011; author of papers, chapters and books on analytic training, practice and institutions and the relation of psychoanalysis and culture.

Gabriela Legorreta is a Training and Supervising Analyst at the Montreal Psychoanalytic Institute and Society (French section of the Canadian Psychoanalytic Society); Director of the Institute of Psychoanalysis of Montreal; President Elect of the Canadian Psychoanalytic Society; Ex-chair and consultant of the IPA Publications Committee; Co-chair of the Study Group Psychoanalytic Bridges with South America; Co-editor with Lawrence Brown of the book *On Freud's Two Principles of Mental Functioning* (2016); Consultant at the Montreal Fertility Center and Coordinator of the Spanish book section of the Advisory Committee on Foreign Language Book reviews of the *Journal of the American Psychoanalytic Association*, private practice.

Ruggero Levy is a Training and Supervising Analyst of the Psychoanalytic Society of Porto Alegre. He is the Former President of SPPA. He was the co-chair for Latin America of the Program Committee of the 53rd IPA Congress, July 2023, Cartagena, Colombia. He was a member of the IPA Board from 2011 to 2013 and from 2013 to 2015. He was the Chair of the IPA Working Parties Committee from 2017 to 2020; professor and supervisor of the Luiz Guedes Study Center of the psychiatry department of UFRGS and the Center for Studies, Care and Research of Childhood and Adolescence (CEAPIA); author of several book chapters and scientific articles published in regional, national and international specialized journals, as well as rapporteur and speaker in several national and international scientific events.

Carlos Moguillansky has an MD and a Master's in Sociology of Culture (UNSAM). He is a trainer and supervisor psychoanalyst of the Buenos Aires Psychoanalytic Association, IPA and former Scientific Secretary and President of APDEBA. During his presidency, the IUSAM Mental Health Institute was founded, which is the first IPA psychoanalytic university institute in Latin America. He is a member of the faculty in The University of Buenos Aires (UBA), USAL and IUSAM and invited Professor in México, Panamá and Brazil. He is a former member of the Board of *The International Journal of Psychoanalysis* and current member of the IPA Publications Committee. He is the author of numerous papers in *Argentine* and foreign journals and of the books *Adolescent Clinic, Latencies, Saying the Impossible* and *Pain and Its Defences*. He participated as author and editor in numerous collective books in Spanish and English.

Clara Nemas is a Training and Supervising Analyst of the APDEBA and member of the IPA and FEPAL. She is a child and adolescent psychoanalyst. She was vice president of Simposio and the scientific chair of APdeBA. She was the chair for the IPA Latin-American International Congress and member of the Asian Pacific Committee and the IPA China Committee. She coordinates the studies of Kleinian developments at the APDEBA and of the continuous education at APDEBA about Meltzer's contributions. She coordinates a study group on the project of becoming a psychoanalyst. She is a member of the IJP. She is the author of various papers published nationally and internationally on the subject of ethics, psychoanalytic technique and early development.

Elena Ortiz Jimenez is a training and supervising psychotherapist at Centro Eleia, Mexico. She has a master's and doctorate degree in Psychoanalytic Psychotherapy and Clinical Psychoanalysis. She received a master's degree in Psychoanalytic Psychotherapy from Universidad Marista, in Yucatán, and she lectures regularly on the doctorate degree in Clinical Psychology at Universidad Santa María la Antigua, in Panamá. She is a member of the Mexican Association Study on Child Retardation and Psychosis (AMERPI). Her publications include the following: *La mente en desarrollo. Reflexiones sobre clínica psicoanalítica* [The Mind in Development. Considerations on Clinical Psychoanalysis] (2011); *Donald Meltzer, Vida onírica. Sueños, mente y pensamiento* [Donald Meltzer, Dream Life. Dreams, Mind and Thought] (2019) and *Donald Meltzer. Actualizaciones en Psicoanálisis, un estudio sobre su obra* [Donald Meltzer. Current Views on Psychoanalysis, a Study of His Work] (2022). She co-edited *Diálogos clínicos en psicoanálisis* [Clinical Dialogues on Psychoanalysis] (2005); *Lo psíquico: fantasía, fantasma y realidad* [The Psyche: Phantasy, Phantasm, and Reality] (2011); *El trauma. Social, familiar, subjetivo* [Trauma. Social, Family and Subjective] (2021) and collaborated on *Las perspectivas del psicoanálisis* [Psychoanalytic Perspectives] (2001).

Carlos Tabbia is a Doctor in Psychology (Univ. of Barcelona); founding member of the Psychoanalytic Group of Barcelona; member of the Argentine Society of Psychoanalysis (SAP-IPA); didactic of the European Federation for Psychoanalytic Psychotherapy (EFPP) and author of the book *The Clinical Comprehension of Meaning: The Bion/Meltzer Vertex* (2021).

Virginia Ungar MD is a Training and Supervising Analyst at the Buenos Aires Psychoanalytic Association (APDEBA). She specializes in child and adolescent analysis. She was the former Chair of the IPA's Child and Adolescent Psychoanalysis Committee (COCAP) and of the Committee for Integrated Training. She received the Platinum Konex Award for Psychoanalysis in 2016. She is the former President of the IPA (2017–2021).

Donald Meltzer at Passover with family in California. 1990's

Introduction

Carlos Moguillansky

The idea of editing this book found its propitious time in the meeting of psychoanalysts that took place in Buenos Aires to commemorate the 100th anniversary of Donald Meltzer's birth. On that occasion, we accepted the invitation of Virginia Ungar and Clara Nemas who organized this event which began with the opening lecture with Meg Harris Williams as the guest speaker. The lecture is published in this book alongside contributors who were interested in transmitting Meltzer's ideas. We are grateful to Virginia Ungar, who helped with her always friendly approach in the creation of this book.

Psychoanalytic work emerged as a dialogical cure which was based on free association of the analysand and free-floating attention of the analyst. This dialogue was intuitively present in Ana O's treatment, which she ironically called the "talking cure". And it was even present in an implicit manner during Sigmund Freud's self-analysis, when he needed the presence and dialogue – would we say transferential today? – of his friend Fliess. Freud took for granted the existence of a listener who would bear witness to and welcome the expression of his emotions and unconscious contents. Dialogue is an expressive support, which forms and receives a thought in action, or rather, an expression that unfolds. Based on the expressive language, the discursive exchange locates and distributes positions and meanings existing among different characters. This happens within the subjective experience and in the dialogues that a person establishes with those close to him. Freud defined this projection of discursive experience as projection and displacement. And M. Klein called projective identification the defensive movement that locates complex aspects of psychic experience in different internal and external localities of the psychic life. Today we would say that talking does not only have the function of communicating, because as Austin (1962) states, "things are done by speaking". Through speaking, experiences are defined, intentions are expressed and promised and conflicts are resolved. This discursive movement of the mind accumulates memory, grows and transforms itself, sometimes imperceptibly and other times through abrupt jumps and catastrophic transformations.

DOI: 10.4324/9781003441861-1

However, we find in the introjective phenomenon one of the keys to psychic functioning. This notion has been studied as a reversion of projection or as the result of identification with models proposed by the family, but neither of these solutions seems satisfactory. The proposal to add terms such as introjective identification is a sign that it has not been possible to find the key to make the distinction between the identification based on the truth of the subject and the mimetic fictions that attempt to emulate the truth of the subject. The post-Kleinian notion of adhesive identification constitutes the first fruitful approach to this issue, since it establishes the difference between adhesive mimesis and identification which recaptures elements of the subject's authenticity.

The notions of filiation and affiliation offer a new approach to the problem of introjection, insofar as affiliation is the linear assumption of a family model and filiation is the result of the person's desire, which illuminates and retroactively creates new ancestors in accordance with this new version of the self. Both filiation and affiliation revolve around the recognition of a core of truth that guarantees the authenticity of the subjective experience. This kernel of truth provides a personal anchorage to the inevitable subjective fiction of any personal experience. It is, therefore, the point of convergence between individual psychology, which pays attention only to the individual, and social psychology that pays attention only to the social world. This nucleus, this point of convergence, exposes the knot between the violent interpretation of the subject's reality, as shown by P. Aulagnier, and the way in which subjective truth resists the demands and violent interpretations emanating from the environment.

From another angle, the discontent created by psychic conflict cannot be avoided. The reader will notice that the authors of the book describe the atmosphere, the intimacy and the emotional aesthetics of a conflictive world still little known. Their descriptions abound in cross-references between the expression of pain and aesthetic experience. Their chapters provide a unique spectrum of versions on this subject and introduce a fruitful debate on the nature of emotion and, in particular, on the link between emotion and aesthetic experience, both in the apprehension of the beauty of the object and its unique emotional functions and in the pain and the psychic defenses associated with it. Meltzer was an active and generous psychoanalyst; and he planted the seed of his thinking in different places in Europe, the USA and Latin America. One hundred years after his birth, the book illustrates a plural vision of his work, in which his theoretical and clinical influence is underlined and aims to highlight the validity and the way in which his work is still presently useful.

The study of this psychoanalytic dialogue sheds light on its main qualities: it is a dialogue characterized by conflict between different psychic instances; it is an intimate exchange, born from the most personal truth of a person. In analytic work, it takes a certain curiosity and boldness to face pain and uncertainty. And, finally, it also takes patience and tolerance in the face of the manifestation of very raw and intense emotions. Without these conditions, analytical dialogue becomes bureaucratic and loses the driving force of a real act that demands a true response and often a passionate decision.

Meltzer says with simplicity that emotional life is an experience akin to the experience in a family. In this way, he refers to the condition of intimate life. This means, in a few words, that intimacy is the natural habitat of the emotional life, because it is the appropriate atmosphere to protect spontaneity. It follows from these simple sentences that intimacy, emotional expression and the protected world of the family are the prerequisites for a vulnerable human being to express his truest and most original condition of his life. Family life provides the necessary conditions for a complex exchange, which distributes the specialized positions and functions of the generations and the sexes. Family has a varied individual expression, but its heterogeneous manifestation aims at resolving the vital development of a new generation, renewed at each peal of life.

Thus, despite its variations, dialogue, especially family dialogue, is not an ordinary exchange. In it, subtle implicit emotional forms are deployed, which shape the very exchange and contribute to the development of its interlocutors.

The psychoanalytic session attempts to generate an intimate atmosphere akin to family life. For it is only under such conditions that the encounter with a hidden truth will occur. The human dialogue that takes place in the family and in the session is above all a dialogue which is not always friendly. Even more, it is colored by conflict, because it reflects the clash between two or more aspects of a divided being. In every family gesture, in every solution to a daily event, the individuals are confronted with the same problem. There are things that can be taught and others that cannot, these must be discovered in the course of life. Meltzer says: *"there are things that can be learned, but they cannot be taught"*. Access to the symbolic register requires learning from one's own experience. You can know several men, but you cannot teach a man to be human. That has to be discovered. One can know a mother, but one must discover motherhood, and so on ... The difference between knowledge and the access to abstract truth unfolds in the experience of all facets of life, from sex to emotionality. In this discovery, there are no shortcuts possible, for the nature of this transformation exceeds a simple accumulation of information.

Being a father or a mother, a man or a woman, an adult or a child requires access to a discovery that goes beyond appearance. With a certain superficiality, one can pretend that such access is possible, but that is a fallacy. Meltzer describes this superficiality as a restriction of the imagination, equivalent to believing that if you wear latex gloves and a mask you are a surgeon. The attention to the direction and movement of psychic functions has been very present in the Kleinian school, from the recommendations of Hanna Segal in Dream, Phantasy and Art (1990), to the ideas previously put forward by Wilfred Bion in *Transformations* (1965). These ideas point, as we saw, to a definition of the introjective function.

Bion described introjection as an incarnation that institutes psychic instances. This discovery modified the goals of psychoanalysis. Its aim is not only to decipher an enigma, to solve a lived pain or a current conflict; it seeks to transform the relationship of psychic forces and to give new ways of coexistence between their instances, in the search for an approach to the truth of the subject. In this sense, the introjective function is a key factor both in the development of psychic life and in the vicissitudes of the analytic cure, since the different destiny of the person's identifications depends on it, both in their nature and in their function. An individual indoctrinated in the emblems of a whole is not the same as a person who is aware and responsible for his own subjective truth.

The conceptual evolution of the relationship between aesthetic experience and pain

The aesthetic experience and the experience of pain were addressed by Sigmund Freud from the beginning in his work about fantasy and about the pain caused by loss and traumatic experiences that were not transformed by adequate elaboration. Freud linked both themes, the aesthetic experience and pain, by giving importance to the oneiric figuration (Freud, S. 1900) and the role of the activity of play in the working through of pain, in general, and in trauma, in particular (Freud, S. 1920). The oneiric figuration posed the challenge of expressing in an imaginary language the symbolic experience threaded in the unconscious, which had its maximum expression in the symptom and in the defensive compromise formations. During that same time, the ideas of imaginary symbolism in art were insinuated, which would culminate with the link between W. Kandinsky and A. Schonberg and the circular letter of Wassili Kandinsky (1912), where he stated the existence of an exchange of languages between literature, pictorial images and music.

Years later, Walter Benjamin (1925) contributed a decisive element with the study of drama – *Trauerspiel* – which unites the ideas of mourning and play in its penumbra of meaning. Baroque drama puts in tension the ideas of myth and allegory. Myth takes the subject out of his vital condition placing him in the role of the hero, the myth does this by changing the reference from the current time of the life of the subject to the narrative time of the myth. Contrary to the myth, allegory breaks down the elements of the fact into a non-idealized distribution, which happens in time as a permanent process. This tension is not gratuitous, for it divides the waters between mythical idealization – proper to the sacred realm and apart from human labor – and the distribution of allegory, which eventually leads to playing and narrative elaboration. This subtle line of division will have consequences in the future. It will mark, on the one hand, the destinies of beliefs and of a fetishistic idealization, and, on the other hand, the destiny of the emotional elaboration through playing and in the life of the group. Here we see the importance of fiction in emotional working through, especially in its use of the distribution of roles and functions of drama, be it playful or not.

Playing is an activity that allows one to combine the experience from the active role of the ludic subject (Freud, S. 1920) and, above all, to link the experience to the register of language. Playing links and communicates the experience both in the direction of the others as well as toward the subject himself. Playing allows for a movement that permits interchanges of the position of the subject and the position of the object. It allows to alternate passive and active roles and to modify the point of perspective of the scene of playing. This gives playing an extraordinary expressive and communicative capacity and makes it an essential tool for defining and redefining emotional life. Its movement modifies the positions of the self in different dramatic configurations. These qualities are also present in the dramatization we encounter in a dream, described by Ella Sharpe and Ernest Jones, as well as in group exchanges, especially in groups with young people. These movements alter the subject's position with respect to his relationship with external reality, but even more significantly, they also alter the subject's relationship with himself.

Donald Meltzer (1973) defined these experiences as variations of the experience of identity, depending on whether this identity is established as a consequence of projective identification, introjection or identification with an aspect of the self. When the truth of the subject approaches the most original zone of the person, what Wilfred Bion called O, these subjective movements can have an abrupt effect. In these cases, the renewed link with O generates an authentic subjective truth, establishing a state of exception which defines a new organization of manners and norms in the psychic life. Bion described this event as a catastrophic change.

Ludic and aesthetic experiences have things in common. Both contain emotional elements, and sensory contact is involved in their experiences. We usually appeal to the aesthetic experience to express or to understand emotions, but it is worth asking if this explains the fact that we identify in them similar aspects that overlap each other. When there is inadequate intra or interpersonal or interpersonal communication, aesthetic metaphor is a necessary, or perhaps indispensable, vehicle to achieve the symbolization of emotional events. Literature and the plastic arts give innumerable examples of how this symbolization to be achieved. However, are we sure that emotional life is an aesthetic experience? This book delves into this question.

Psychic life expresses itself through different means. Freud stated that dreams have figurative resources which do not have a precise symbolic function that helps express traumatic experiences. Freud's approach emphasizes the complexity of the function of representation which transcends any simple nomination or figuration. Freud understands, based on his ideas on double inscription, that representation requires a full investment between the unconscious images and the words that attempt to represent them in the system preconscious. One could extend this idea and consider transferential repetitions as a fractal model of the way Freud considered the work of dreams. These repetitions reiterate and provide a figure to a form, an experiential experience or a cliché that, in its abstraction, indicates the existence of experiences that have not been elaborated. Would it be taking the idea too far to think that the elaboration of these experiences includes an elaboration of pain? Or that pain is lessened in the course of this elaborative transformation? Pain seems to find an elaborative refuge in its relation to dramatization and in language.

M. Klein contributed a description of depressive anxiety. She provided details on the destinies and defensive resources of this experience. After M. Klein, Wilfred Bion's study on the passionate intricacy of the bonds of curiosity, love and hate was decisive. On this line of thought, Donald Meltzer studied the relation between the aesthetic experience and tyranny. The reader will find references to these themes in Bion's *Transformations* (1965 [1984]) and Donald Meltzer's *Apprehension of Beauty* (2008) and *Sexual States of Mind* (1973). In both cases, the descriptions of the different concepts rely on the relationship of extreme dependence of the child on an object of vital importance. In a more clinical description, the infant bonds with its mother's gaze and maintains a stable and firm gaze connection. If this does not happen, the child's gaze goes astray. What does the child find in this vital encounter? It is difficult to say that the child finds an object, since this expressive act cannot be described as mere objectivity. By defining the fellow human being as an object, the radical difference between a material object and a human being is lost. The desire of the fellow human being is offered as a subjective act that meets the desire of the child. When this happens, a meeting of subjectivities takes place. This detail is not minor, since it will have an important impact on the emotional consequences that will be repeated throughout the child's life. This fact is of unquestionable importance for the analytic situation and finds its expression in the analytic transference.

Expectations of a positive meeting of subjectivities are probably not fulfilled in most cases. And reality, whether imposed or absent, prevails over subjective expectation. It is known that abuse occurs when the desire of another is imposed on the subject's desire. Reality imposes its violence. And this is portrayed with expressive objectivity. The abused child draws with extreme objectivity the genitalia of the abuser. The objectivity of mimesis expresses the violence of the real encounter and, therefore, expresses in his copy the violence incurred on his desire. We should ask ourselves if this objective way of expression is also found in other violent encounters.

Tolerance to violence is usual and happens on a daily basis and is not far from public life. Private life aims to escape from that violence. Where one can find experiences marked with a greater subjective modulation that protects oneself from being exposed to the pain that characterizes a violent and insensitive encounter of subjectivities. This is the role of intimacy in private emotional exchanges. Intimate life tends to develop less violent encounters in spite of the fact that violence reappears in these encounters whenever there is pain.

The analytic concept of trauma describes the real violence of uncontrolled desire – one's own or someone else's – of a fellow human being, of a natural event or of the subject himself. This violence devastates the subjective anticipation; the individual was unable to anticipate it. The violence gets registered as an objective act, where the objectivity of the event violates the subjectivity of the victim. In a few words, it violates his human condition. This record in the psyche has a mimetic quality, lacking poetry, since it does not provide any opportunity for the subject to exercise his creative dimension. What is lacking is poetry, poetry that provides a subjective addition and dimension to the event which will transform it into experience. This will end up in an admirable construction between the new and real of the event and the expectation the subject had of it. Once again, fiction provides that quota of elaboration that mitigates the pain of a too violent or insensitive encounter.

The experience of beauty: between the apprehension of free beauty and the domain of the sensory

The experience of beauty develops within an awkward confusion between the apprehension of the priceless and enigmatic beauty of the good object and the encounter with the fecal exchange of goods and cultural goods – the cultural goods. The goods can be traded, to the point of constituting living currencies susceptible to be treasured. The good object umbilicates within itself toward an enigma where what is new is the expression of its freedom. At the other extreme, in the realm of possessive goods, the new is opposed to the obsolete, in a renewed greed for the latest model of the object. Once again, what is new oscillates between the surprise of the emotional event and the radiance of the consumable object. Emotion differs from the consumable object, but the culture industry offers operative systems and consumable objects that are proposed as confusing substitutes for the emotional experience.

Hanna Segal, in *Dream, Phantasy and Art* (1990) distinguishes psychic processes according to their regressive or developmental direction. This direction corresponds to the type of relationship and the nature of the objects and the self in each defensive situation. The changes of direction of a psychic process are, therefore, a way of describing the type of motivation at play in each of its expressions, ranging from intense passive dependence to possessive and tyrannical manipulation of the object's freedom. In simple terms, the question of freedom and tyrannical defense is located in the midpoint between subjective events and the omnipotent manipulation that transforms them into objects of practical domination. This confusion prevents distinguishing a similar other from an inanimate object and treats and permutes them as if they were equivalent disregarding the essential fact that the human condition develops around desires and feelings, providing, as a consequence, an experience quite different from what is offered by a simple object.

A similar fact occurs when one identifies the abstract quality of a definite object: the divinity of a god, the beauty of a beautiful object, etc. That elusive and enigmatic dimension is at the edge of repressive experience. And perhaps Jacques Lacan's approach to the difference between the specular object and the object of the drive provides an adequate possible explanation to this question. The image of the object is formed within its imaginary, even specular, silhouette. However, the outline of the silhouette is already the first abstraction necessary to define the leap that occurs from the imaginary register to the symbolic one, which allows the capacity to conceive the absence of the object, like Bion's suggestive description of *"the place that the object used to occupy"*. The reader will understand the situation if he remembers that the Greeks and Romans were aware of the absence of something, but they did not have the notion of the arithmetical zero, which was a symbolic achievement of the Middle Ages.

However, repression brings into play a different situation. The object of the drive is outside the field of the mirroring experience and is defined by having a drive attribution. In other words, to speak of the object of the drive is a doubtfully objective way of describing a libidinal attribution. Taking into consideration all these elements, it will be possible to advance our understanding of the role of beauty in the construction of the good object. In *Transformations*, Wilfred Bion (1984) distinguishes the difference between the encounter with a *god* and the incarnation of *divinity* in man. That distinction provides a double distinction, between the direction of the link – the symmetrical encounter with a god and the asymmetrical inspiration with divinity – along with two modes of referring to the divine. This double distinction marks both the nature of the link as well as the nature of those who participate in it: men and the sacred.

In fact, it was perhaps Donald Meltzer who provided the conceptual elements that allowed him to identify the confusion between nourishing and fecal objects, described in anal masturbation. Once again, we are confronted here with the difference in nature of two different objects and two different types of links: one with a nutritive object, enigmatic and free, and another one with a fecal object, which can be dominated at will. This confusion between the two objects and their respective links is confirmed in the current use of cultural operative systems that attempt to replace and reproduce an emotional experience. These systems deny the essential difference between the respect for the freedom of an emotional experience and the mastery of sensory experiences that are similar to emotional experience only in appearance.

These differences will develop two modes of relation that the human being will have with the world: one is presided over by the asymmetrical helplessness in relation to the object that provides assistance with what is necessary to survive and develop; the other mode of relation corresponds to the idealization – of a divine object – or of the power over an object that can be dominated at will. The confusion between the two leads to the idealization of the fecal substances, which is elevated to the role of a nourishing object. This confusion reveals the boundary between the introjective dependence on the assisting object and the possessive tyranny, both of the idealized object and of the enslaved object. The latter will be dealt with in the chapter on possessiveness and the claustrophobic phenomena associated with it.

The transferential memory of the emotional encounter with a beautiful object is a frequently observed fact, at least in the advanced stages of psychoanalysis. The beauty that emerges in such a memory is different from that which was described as a cultural consumption, for it does not have the character of a social commonplace. It is characterized by its individual and idiosyncratic nature. The person has difficulty in sharing with other people, among them with the analyst, the mysterious experience of beauty ascribed to the encounter with a person. The encounter is seen as a beautiful event, it is strongly associated with an image: his or her face, his or her gaze, his or her light, etc. It seems to be the effect of an encounter of glances or of an emotional exchange, similar to what happens between a mother and her baby. The memory awakens an intense experience of love and trusting surrender to an idealized person who is everything to the subject. The rapturous aesthetic experience installs an intense emotional dependence. It is a visual, auditory, tactile, kinesthetic, odorous or gustatory experience. In all cases, the intense emotion predominates, as something personal and private. It is something non-transferable. No one can take away this fact, this feeling of self – *Selbstgefühl* – that founds the Ego. The beautiful scene is linked to that very thing that founds the "I". It is partly a reproduction of what has been experienced and much more the creation of that experience in itself. Arnold Schönberg said: *one paints a picture, not what it represents.* That subjective identity, of the subject with himself including his feeling of himself, it gets distinguished from the idea of an object, even more so if this object is experienced as a similar one, as another person. For this reason, the experience of this beautiful scene is at the center and origin of one's own experience of self. However, the symmetrical identity of the I with its *Selbstgefühl* finds in the unconscious its own dynamic contradiction. And this is the key point of any psychoanalytic approach, insofar as this experience has an ostensive and indefinable dimension, which sinks its roots in the mysterious labyrinths of the unconscious. The gaze of that mother fuses in a single image the fullest surrender of love with the most elusive mystery of her freedom. This double face of the experience gives rise both to the belief in the unconditionality of love and to the concern of an eventual fading of the Ego, in the face of the freedom of desire, both one's own and that of the other.

Plutarch (Ziegler, K. 1949 [1965]) in his description of the goddess Isis with her face veiled by a canvas offers an appropriate image that helps illustrate what has just been developed. The scene accords with the myth of an enigma – *ainigma*. "*In Sais the statue of Athena seated, whom they also consider Isis, had an inscription like this: 'I am all that has been, what is and will be and my people never lifted by any mortal'*" (Plutarco, Isis and Osiris: 73). Plutarch refers to Neith, goddess of Sais in the Nile Delta. She is considered the asexual creator of the world. Herodotus equated Neith with Athena and, later, with Isis. This belief sustains the principle involved in the myth of a virginal and asexual, divine and mysterious creator. This myth must not be revealed so as not to mix the pure – immortal – with the impure – mortal. The taboo of maternal virginity and the sacred need to omit sexuality is seen in the Marian cult and in the Jewish and Muslim prohibition to represent the divine. That sacred *religio* presides over the unconscious caesura and provides a model of the veiled in language. Horror is veiled. And the sexual impulse is covered with a cloak of repression. The result is an ambiguous and contradictory expression that both Burke and Kant defined with the idea of the sublime, as an aesthetic effect of that beautiful, enigmatic, distressing and horrifying mystery.

In other words: how to reconcile the idea of a beautiful experience at the center of the experience of the Ego along with its inevitable inconsistency, each time it falls under the fading that accompanies the return of the repressed? Each of these two aspects of the Ego has its own autonomy and, therefore, falls into inevitable conflict with each other. This dialectic of the Ego with the masters who suppress it is part of daily life and of its inevitable psychopathology, every time the Ego is confronted with its slavery to reality to its jokes, its forgetfulness, its lapsus linguae, its missteps and its erroneous acts, in this alternation between its laughter and its horror at its surprising occurrences. In the appearance of the unconscious, the Ego encounters the most alien of itself. Paul Ricoeur would say that it is a question of another of oneself, which emerges as the most improper of its being. Therein lies men's tendency to neurosis and his need to appeal to his wildest beliefs.

These beliefs emerge as the best projective explanation of experiences that have a complete understanding. They have a strong emotional charge and provide intense certainty. They preserve the unity of the self, in its worldview of an established order. Belief is an exoskeleton that sustains the worldview and preserves the Ego from possible collapse.

Mutilated objects and tyranny

In *Sexual States of Mind*, Meltzer offers a subtle description of fanaticism and tyranny.

Psychic life proposes an exalted apprehension of the beauty of the object. Behind that exalted and beautiful contact nestles a human element and the beginnings of an emotional component. The emotion and the beauty of the object announce its goodness only if that object is at the same time good. In contrast to such beauty, an exchange of mutilated objects is proposed, which have lost precisely the beautiful and emotional condition of the primordial contact with the object – what we mean as the human condition.

The idea of a mutilated object carries an ingredient of pain and guilt, which is the result of a cruel act on a fellow human being. This pain, inevitably anonymous, is exchanged through a projection, which disproves and relieves the subject of the guilt experienced for the pain suffered. This defense, far from lessening the guilt, increases it. And, in the end, it ends up in a severe split, which divides self-idealized and denigrated aspects that are accused of having inflicted that damage. Someone must take the blame: a relative, a neighbor or a stranger. The scapegoat is sought and found. It assumes the accusation of being the great culprit of individual or social pain. We are witnesses of this social maneuver, usual and current, that resolves in Isaac, in Christ or in an anonymous being the strange pact of alliance with a solution as sacred as singular. One will be the chosen one only if there is a goat to atone for the alien that falls outside oneself, that stranger must be removed from the core of us, of each individual and of the social being. Meltzer adds that, even in the most successful psychoanalysis, a schizophrenic element remains split from the individual. And with him, nightmares of terror and fear will plague his dreams. This is a renewed reference to the Freudian bedrock.

References

Austin, J. L. (1962): *How to do things with words. The William James lectures,* Oxford.

Benjamin, W. (1925): *Ursprung des deutschen Trauerspiels.* Berlin, Rowohlt Verlag, 1928.

Bion, W. (1965): *Transformations, from learning to growth.* Maresfield Libraries, London, Karnak, 1984.

Freud, S. (1900): *Traumdeutung. Über den Traum. Gesammelte Werke,* Bd. 2/3.

Freud, S. (1920): *Jenseits des Lustprinzip.* Leipzig, Int. Psych. Verlag, 1921. *Gesammelte Werke,* Bd. 13.

Kandinsky, W. (1912): *Rückblick.* Paris, Maeght Editeur, 1951.

Meltzer, D. (1973): *Sexual states of mind.* London. Karnac.

Meltzer, Donald and Williams, Meg Harris. (2008): *The apprehension of beauty: The role of aesthetic conflict in development, art and violence.* The Harris Meltzer Trust. London. Karnac.

Plutarco (circa s. I after C): *Isis y Osiris*. Trad. F. Palomino Pardo. Ed. Gredos, Madrid, 1995.

Segal, H. (1990): *Dream, phantasy and art*. London, Routledge.

Ziegler, K (1949): *Plutarchos von Chaironea*, Stuttgart, 1949 = Plutarco (trad. it. de M. R. Zancan Rinaldini), Brescia, 1965. Also in R. Flaceliére *Plutarque. Oeuvres Morales I*, París, 1987.

1 Psychoanalysis as a form of art

Working with Donald Meltzer

Meg Harris Williams

Introduction[1]

Donald Meltzer always thought of psychoanalysis as an art-science, in which the practice was an art, and the findings those of a science: He wrote:

> If the practice of psychoanalysis is an art, as I firmly believe, and its findings are those of a descriptive science, it is essential that it be done by individuals who can think for themselves.[2]

The growing body of knowledge about the mind evolves in a spiral manner, in which new phenomena are observed that expand the existing model of the mind, and this, in turn, enables new observations to be made that could not be seen before. This is 'thinking for ourselves' and it is an art form.

The post-Kleinian view of the way in which we learn to 'think for ourselves' is an object-related one. Bion said 'our minds are made up for us by forces about which we know nothing', but to say this is already to know something: it is to know that our internal objects proceed in a mysterious way and our choice is to follow (into the depressive position) or to substitute (in a paranoid-schizoid way). Meltzer always considered that these mysterious processes were in fact observable and describable, if one was careful to avoid premature explanations. The symbols that result from dreamwork and unconscious thinking are observable, as they are in art forms, and they are created in an analogous way, even if not identical (primarily owing to their private rather than public significance). Often indeed these symbols include imaginative representations of the objects themselves, especially the 'combined object' that originates from the underlying phantasy of creative parental figures.

Thinking for oneself, or 'becoming' oneself as Bion puts it, means learning to be faithful to these internal directors, just as the poets and artists describe following their Muse. It is what Milton meant when he said his ambition was to 'be a true Poem' – not to become perfect but to serve these

DOI: 10.4324/9781003441861-2

inspiring forces, and to follow the ideal of Beauty 'through all the shapes and forms of things'.

For Meltzer, this is also the way psychoanalysis works: its goal is not to create a preconceived picture of a respectable personality, but to set in motion the innate organic shaping of the self by internal objects, and it does this by means of what he calls a 'conversation between internal objects' – of the analyst, and the analysand. The transference relationship (which he says is by no means restricted to psychoanalysis) has the capacity to revive and relive the prototypal mother-infant relationship, learning to think through emotional reciprocity with the object.

He called psychoanalysis a 'forcing-house for symbol formation'[3] and considered the process of coming-to-knowledge through symbols of emotional experience to be not just artistic but beautiful. Unlike some, he does not split the idea of beauty from that of creativity or symbol formation. The process is a beautiful one even when the psychic organisation it reveals may be ugly or distorted – it is the beauty of truth. This is inseparable from the Kleinian view of reparation of or rather by internal objects. The therapeutic value of the process is entirely dependent on a recognition, conscious or unconscious, of its beauty despite the painful feelings associated with aesthetic conflict – love and hate of the object. When Bion asks in his *Memoir* 'Could Beauty help?'[4] Meltzer's answer is an emphatic yes, and also a demonstration.

Meltzer often described his own counter-dreaming processes, such as sitting in Plato's cave watching the shadows on the wall, or watching for intuitive flashes like deers'-tails in the dark, or listening to the music of the analytic conversation and noting his own response, since it is the music – over and above the lexical significance of an interpretation – which the patient hears. These features of artistic method, or similar ones, have since been adopted and echoed by others and were intimated by Bion especially in his *Memoir*; but Meltzer is also characterised by his vision of the 'natural history' of the psychoanalytic process – in a way analogous to the making of a work of art through symbolic structures. Each individual analysis contributes not just to an improved, more complex, more ethically sophisticated mental structure (in both patient and analyst), but also to an expanded model of the mind which is the more public result of the artistic method.

I have been asked to say a little about how my own work as a literary critic together with Meltzer. He always said his talent was for reading dreams; mine was for reading poetry. It was a kind of interdigitation that began a long way back. Although Meltzer had had a love of art since his own childhood, when he went on a European tour with his parents, he was not especially interested in literature although he had certain favourite dramatists – Brecht, Pinter, Miller. Meltzer married my mother after my father Roland Harris died (he was a poet and teacher) and then became immersed in the environment of our literary family and fascinated by the English poets that my sister and I were studying. In the context of individual writing and family discussion, the links between psychoanalysis and literature began to be evaluated in a natural way – it was not an academic exercise. The ghost of my father was also present, I could say. Only later did I learn that he and Meltzer were working together on a study of linguistics and language development, some of whose content is included in the book *Dream Life* in the sections on symbol formation and deep grammar. At that time Meltzer said to me that any intimate relationship, personal or work, must depend on finding objects in common. My father had expressed the same idea in one of his early poems:

> We are of those blessed lovers
>   Who loved before they knew,
> Without pursuit or fleeing;
>   And met as pilgrims do,
>
> Whose eyes, bent on the going,
>   Turn once to ask the day
> And find their end's companion
>   Going the same road as they.[5]

The 'same road' is that of aesthetics – and its role in life's pilgrimage. Other shadowy figures, of course, were also present – Meltzer has mentioned how he found a suitable internal psychic partner for Mrs Klein, namely the naturalist and philosopher of organic growth Darcy Wentworth Thompson. On my side there was also my remarkable schoolteacher Joie Macaulay, whom Meltzer considered a mysterious phenomenon owing to her 'passion for literature'; with hindsight I now attribute certain moments that emerged even from the days of my own analysis when I somehow conveyed her ambience, as marking the sowing of seeds of later collaboration. One moment, for example, was when he said that the main division in psychoanalysis was between those who thought that mental events were real, and those who thought Mrs Klein's language was purely metaphorical and the idea of the 'inner world' just a matter of phraseology. There were parallels here between the study of literature and of psychoanalysis – is literary interpretation just a language game or an attempt to describe the psychic reality of one's own response.

At one point I quoted, from my school lessons, Coleridge's 'Such is the life, such the form', being the guiding principle of the Cambridge school of 'Practical Criticism' in which I was reared by Miss Macaulay. There, too, Meltzer found a kind of structural analogy with psychoanalytic practice. Practical Criticism entails a type of close reading of poetic diction and formal structures that is designed to note the movements of the 'deep grammar' of an emotional situation – the signs beneath the lexical surface significance – the 'art symbol' as Susanne Langer defines it. As such it is analogous to close observation in the analytic consulting room, the training for which was developed by Esther Bick's method of infant observation and then developed further by my mother Martha Harris into a full training programme at the Tavistock. Simple and obvious though it is, the role of observation is so often sidelined (because it is so difficult) in any art or science – and theories and interpretations are substituted, as Bion so often lamented.

Meltzer often cited the philosopher of aesthetics Susanne Langer, who differentiates between 'presentational form' and 'discursive form'.[6] Discursive form is the superficial level of interpretation, the straightforward lexical connotation like a medical diagnosis. Presentational form describes the deep grammar (as it is called in literary criticism), the symbol with all its sensuous qualities, which contains meaning in a three-dimensional way and cannot simply be paraphrased, although it can be described. Meltzer introduced me to Langer and the Wittgenstein-Cassirer tradition, which I realised was actually a continuation of the Coleridgean-Kantian neo-Platonic philosophy of aesthetic experience followed by the great poets. Langer says it is characteristic of all art forms to present in symbolic form not just 'feelings' but 'the life of feeling' (that is, the dynamic for developmental thinking), a philosophy parallel to Bion's theory of thinking. Meltzer also introduced me to the work of Adrian Stokes, who provided a model for aesthetic criticism in Kleinian terms that I named 'symbolic congruence' – the reader's counter-dream.[7]

It was my mother, a very non-shadowy presence, who encouraged Meltzer to take Bion's work seriously (he was previously suspicious of him, but came to find in his work theoretical reinforcement for his own belief in the predominance of 'the aesthetic' in psychoanalysis). She presided over and knitted together the links between Mrs Bick's infant observation, literature and psychoanalysis, in the way Meltzer described her knitting jumpers to keep everyone in a good temper during the filming of Bion's *Memoir* in India.[8] As he wrote on the jacket cover of *The Apprehension of Beauty*, for which he asked me to write two chapters (on *Hamlet* and on literary criticism):

> This volume has grown over the years almost as a family project of Martha Harris, her two daughters Meg and Morag and her husband, Donald Meltzer. It therefore has its roots in English literature and its branches waving wildly about in psychoanalysis. Its roots in English literature – Shakespeare, Milton, Wordsworth, Keats, Coleridge and Blake – are as strong as the psycho-analytical branching from Freud, Klein and Bion. Its philosophical soil is certainly Plato, Russell, Whitehead, Wittgenstein, Langer, Cassirer and, in aesthetics, Adrian Stokes.[9]

Gradually all these points of interest, guided by their inspiring figures, focused and fused in support of Meltzer's innate belief in psychoanalysis as an art form.

In the mid-1970s, I was working on my thesis *Inspiration in Milton and Keats*, which became my first book and the basis for all my books: it was a study, based on analysis of poetic diction, of different modes of identification in poetic influence and poetic identity. Meltzer said to me, this book is really about aesthetics; and in a sense that statement demarcated the scope and direction of subsequent work – everything was subsumed under aesthetics. He wrote for the jacket cover:

> Literary criticism has often been taxed with a lack of psychological insight while psychologists, and perhaps psychoanalysts in particular, when writing about literature, have been accused of being beside the point, aesthetically. This book explores the nature of creative thought, through its focal concern with the phenomenon of inspiration. It approaches the works and lives of Milton and Keats from two directions, and with a dual purpose. Equipped with both formal and informal training in literature, art and psychology, the author has mounted a most complex and fascinating attack on this long-avoided problem: is the Muse a formal figure of speech or a psychological reality?[10]

He thought literary criticism was itself an art form not merely an academic exercise (as viewed by Oxford), in the same way as psychoanalysis had to be an art form in order to perform its dual function – discovering more about the mind and rescuing the lost children of the personality. The mind of the analyst had to investigate itself at the same time as that of the patient, just as in aesthetic criticism (in any field) the critic's response is a type of countertransference to the emanations of the art-symbol. It is not an arbitrary subjective response attributing its own vision to the art-symbol, but a structural readjustment of the mind. Coleridge described this as the instantaneous identity of the subjective and the objective in the 'life of ideas'.

Meltzer appreciated the early work of Hanna Segal on symbol formation but thought it did not develop further. His own work is not so much 'a psychoanalytic approach to aesthetics' as a vision of psychoanalysis as a new branch of aesthetics. Aesthetics subsumes psychoanalysis; as it does literary criticism, and all art forms. What is new is that personality development is also seen as an aesthetic activity, governed by the activation of the sense of beauty – something new to psychoanalytic thinking but traditional and quite explicit in poetry. In a complementary way, the traditional poetic relation of poet and muse gains a psychological validity in terms of Kleinian object relations, which was the subject of my book *The Vale of Soulmaking*, the last of my books that he read, near the end of his life. In his Foreword he wrote that these internal gods are 'the superior, most evolved segment of the human mind, and their evolution takes place in advance of the self', and that '*The Vale of Soulmaking* promises to become the text for post-Kleinian thought... and the upshot of it all is to establish Mrs Klein as the first "post-Kleinian"'.[11] Of course, the term 'post-Kleinian' has, since then, been used in different ways. But it is worth noting that Meltzer did not see it as in any way going 'beyond' Klein, but rather, as a way of better defining Mrs Klein's own analytic practice, which he regarded as essentially equivalent to that of the poets.

The poet, like the analysand and also the analyst, is not a primary creator but a follower of guidance from internal objects whose messages are interpreted through symbol formation. This is what is meant by being an artist. For as Langer says, the advantage that symbols have over sign-language is that they can transcend the interpretant's existing knowledge. Coleridge said, an idea cannot be apprehended except in the form of a symbol. Symbols are vehicles for new ideas and, by nature, are seeded in a psychic state of not-knowing, as in the modern view of psychoanalysis.

To be an artist, in Meltzer's view, is to be impressed by both the beauty and the attacks on beauty that fill the world around us. Where there is aesthetic there is also anti-aesthetic: there are substitute symbols. The poet or artist has always, throughout history, been obsessed with whether their art is 'true' or 'false'; and often, unsure initially which it is. Is their symbol shaped by themselves or by their internal object, the muse? Only the latter has reality, although virtuosic talent can disguise the distinction. The question in psychoanalytic terms is whether the depressive or paranoid-schizoid orientation is dominant. The perpetual drama of the depressive and paranoid schizoid positions – taking the form of true art versus false art – is the subject of most world literature. But it is not only the universal, underlying theme of the protagonists; it is also the internal drama of the poet who, in the vicissitudes of symbol formation, has an infinite interest in the subtle machinations of the 'devil within' and its attempt to hijack creativity. Whatever the surface subject of the work may be, its underlying subject is always this drama of object relations, and it takes the form of self-made symbols versus object-made symbols. Object-made symbols are often displeasing or disturbing at first, until time has revealed their worth; self-made symbols are often fashionable and appeal to basis assumptions about how we ought to look and feel, in a given moment in a given society. All forms of substitute art, pseudo-art, narcissistic display masquerading as art, etc, fall into this category of retreat from aesthetic conflict, the confusion intensified by the beauty of the breast.

And this applies as much to the analytic process as to the analysand's own struggle. Dreams, he says, can be read 'pornographically' as can artworks. An interpretation constitutes an action if it colludes with a pornographic (excitable) rather than a contemplative mode of viewing the dream. Again, this is avoiding the aesthetic conflict demanded by symbol formation and substituting a true symbol with a false one. When Meltzer expanded on his 'Anal masturbation' paper in order to write *The Claustrum*, he asked me to contribute a literary example from *Macbeth*, to specifically illustrate the destruction of thought processes through fake-imaginative equivocation.[12]

Symbolic congruence

Symbols, unlike the language of the already-known, have 'possibility' as
Louise Bourgeois said, or as Emily Dickinson put it:

> I dwell in Possibility –
> A fairer house than Prose –
> More numerous of Windows –
> Superior—for doors –[13]

They contain meaning, beyond that previously known to the artist. They
are not paraphraseable. In psychoanalysis, as in art forms, the quest for
symbol formation begins at the dream-level and is founded on reading
the dream. It is the 'reading' that is complicated – listening to the message
from the objects; formulating it is secondary. Meltzer's view of 'dream life'
as a continuum that is 'sampled periodically' in the consulting room is
different from the older view of the unconscious as a chaotic system. He
focuses rather on the quality of the dream, which can vary through a spectrum from dull-derivative day residue, to condensed, rich and imaginative as in the basis for an artwork with its aspiration to become beautiful.
He writes of the varied qualities of dream life in a way very similar to literary criticism, concentrating on structural qualities; thus dream life and
individual dreams consist of:

> a number of formal structures… drawn up into juxtapositions to cre-
> ate a space scintillating with potentiated meaning. Sometimes words
> and visual forms are seen to interact… At other times spaces are being
> created as containers of meaning. At other times the movements from
> one type of space to another, and the emotional difficulties of making
> such moves, are made apparent.[14]

Such a stream-of-unconsciousness allows for the fact that not all dreams
necessarily have an aesthetic character in themselves. Nonetheless if mental movements, spaces, linkages and closures are to have any aesthetic
quality, it will have its foundations here – in dream-life. For dreams, Meltzer said, are how we deal with our aesthetic experience; they embody our
absorption of – or locate our turning away from – the beauty of the world
and its manifestations.

The ancient Greeks grouped dreams into those that came through the
gates of horn or the gates of ivory – differentiating them as being either
prophetic or misleading. As an alternative to the twin gates, dreams could
be categorised according to how developed their aesthetic quality may be.
The greater the poetic quality of the dream, the more integrated the scin-
tillation between the various different senses and the more poetic it becomes, in the sense of fusing the visual, verbal and musical elements. The

crucial distinction is between dreams which are repetitive evacuations (for this is the psychic state of the dreamer) and dreams which embody an integrated understanding, shaped by the gods.

> Our first striving is towards order, for the material impinges on us as analysts in just as confusing and 'meaningless' a way `as it does on the waking dreamer himself – probably more so. But this striving is not to put order into the chaos of the dream, for that has its own order. Rather we seek to put order into the confusion in our own minds...[15]

The initial impact is one of not-knowing – to the degree that Bion describes the analyst as repeatedly in the position of a new-born infant. It is the simultaneous self-analysis, the internal dialogue with the object, that reveals the meaning, or aesthetic order, of the dream – not precisely the one had by the patient, but the symbolic congruence of a dreamed response.

The analytic conversation

Meltzer says that the analytic work is done by the transference from internal objects 'which enables us to seem to perform functions for the patient that are essential to the development of their thinking'.[16] He says the analytic pair aim at a 'congruence' in their phantasy, so that – as he often put it in later years – there can be a 'conversation between their internal objects'. What sort of conversation is this?

The analyst's unconscious (and conscious) intentionality is the key to whether psychoanalysis is being used solely as a sign-language or as a symbolic one – Bion's 'language of achievement'. It is possible to imagine a hypothetical scenario where the same words might be said but with a different underlying meaning. Martha Harris speaks of the 'enabling' interpretation – as distinct from the correct one – meaning, the interpretation that enables the patient to proceed with the next stage in their thinking.[17] (Coleridge calls this reactivating the spirit of growth.) Whether psychoanalytic interpretation is enabling or dogmatic (end-stopping) is something not visible to anybody but the analyst, who has to look inward for 'the intention that he discerns within himself'.[18] An enabling interpretation is founded on symbolic congruence with the patient's dream – something that stems from the empathy or 'imagining-into' (Keats) of which poets provide such prime examples.

There are different views of what is happening in the analytic conversation. The most popular is probably the 'intersubjective' model that implies literally a merging of minds, based on the fantasy of a mythical state of oceanic oneness, which is equated with artistic intuition. This is essentially a flow-of-libido model with the ideal of homeostasis and dissolution of boundaries, rather than an object-relations model. In the post-Kleinian model with its prenatal extension, there is no merging or oneness; object relations begin with the complementary roles of sperm and ovum and are always a dialogue based on a process of projection and introjection. Imaginative or artistic intuition is based on countertransference, not on merging with the personality of another. The blurring of identities based on a phantasy of original oneness is liable to disguise intrusiveness, the illusion of manipulating the object (or the patient) from within, or even a *folie a deux*.

Symbolic congruence, however, refers to the movement of projective and introjective processes that defines a structural change and reorganisation. It applies to the relation between art forms, as well as to the internal conversation between self and object that takes place within an art form. The projective movements are communicative, questing ones, not omnipotent ones designed to control the object. As Stokes puts it, the art-viewer first loses his separateness and then regains it, but in a changed form, 'as he absorbs the stable self-inclusiveness of the art object'.[19] In this way, not only does the final shape of the work of art become known, but also the developmental thrust of its author's mind become introjected. But the lack of instant understanding, such as that which often happens when reading literature, lead to defensive reactions against experiencing aesthetic conflict. As Bion says, if it is difficult to read literature, how difficult is it to read people.

Meltzer's aesthetic conflict is Bion's alignment with O (reality /the object), not a merging but an intersection or a 'psyche-lodgement',[20] a sharp disturbance, a psychic pregnancy where the existing structure of the mind is invaded by a new seed of growth, contained in a symbol. Meltzer sees the moment of symbol formation as feeling 'cruel', and in a sense being cruel,[21] as the meaning is captured inescapably, and the truth can no longer be blurred, substituted or otherwise evaded by clever lies and manipulations.

The craft of psychoanalysis

Meltzer liked to think of psychoanalysis as a craft whose methods were still evolving in sophistication, by contrast with the wealth of experience already acquired by the arts over many generations. Near the very end of his life he said 'that's what it's all about – the craft'. (This was in the context of remembering my father's book for schoolchildren *The Craft of Verse*, which the publishers had idiotically titled *Poetry for You* thinking it would sell better.) He also said the craft was essentially, and in a way simply, the art of human communication – sensitive, not overbearing, respectful of the other, mindful of boundaries, distinguishing between privacy and secrecy.

He always emphasised the 'musical deep grammar' of the psychoanalytic dialogue, together with the negative capability required to heighten sensitivity to its communications. Reading the deep grammar entails

taking into account matters such as intuition, posture, nuance and res-
onance, 'temperature and distance', the balance between 'routine and inspired interpretation'.[22] He speaks of initial or background 'ruminative
interpretations' whose function is to 'facilitate emergence' of the material
rather than to pin down its significance. Beyond this, and extending the
inquiry, is the 'poetic function' which 'finds the metaphoric means of describing the inner world through the forms of the external world'.

The analyst's craft consists in facilitating the analytic process as a container for symbols; his primary role is to manage the setting, not to manage the analysand.

> But perhaps to state [this] as if the analyst were the container misses
> the point that it is the fitting together of the analyst's attention and
> attitudes to the cooperativeness of the patient that forms and seals the
> container, lending it the degree of flexibility and resilience required
> from moment to moment.[23]

Meltzer's description of 'fitting attention to co-operation' has similarities
with Bion's image of the diamond-cutter who intensifies the diamond's
brilliance by virtue of reflecting the light back along the same route.
The pathway to knowledge is a function of reciprocity. The cutter, like
the analyst, merely opens the pathway; the insight is a function of the
light itself, described by Milton as invoking the heavenly light to 'shine
inwards'.

The container whose boundaries allow the symbol to take shape is
something beyond both partners, created by a 'conversation between internal objects', not by either party on their own, nor even both together
in their ordinary egotistical selves. In this conversation, the 'music of the
countertransference, says Meltzer, is 'absolutely what the patient hears'.[24]
It may be in the tone of voice, but mostly the music is, as Keats puts it, a
'ditty of no tone'[25] – or as Bion would put it, 'atonement':[26] it is essentially
an abstract conversation that goes beyond the identities of the couple, and
they are both babies, listening together to their individual internal reveries, not knowing the answer until the symbol takes shape.

And each time that the 'underlying pattern' (Bion) becomes visible,
or symbol formation takes place, the experience of the analysis as aesthetic object is reinforced. Although for Meltzer, the weaning process is
when this is most evident, it is – from the time of the establishment of
the infantile transference – known to be such, as a form of preconception,
though this knowledge may be denied or buried. This is in line with the
aesthetic conflict, where the experience of beauty and the finding of the
first aesthetic object – the breast – is primary, and the clouding-over with
paranoid-schizoid distrust is secondary. The hope of rediscovery of that
first 'dazzle of the sunrise' – Wordsworth's 'trailing clouds of glory' – is what
sustains the whole endeavour (*The Apprehension of Beauty*, p. 28). And, in

aesthetic conflict, it is inseparable from the awareness of separation. This, like all inspiring processes, is not something that is achieved once and for all, any more than the `depressive position' is a badge or qualification. It is something that has to be continually renewed when each new idea sends its premonitions over the horizon of consciousness – the `shadow of the future' as Bion puts it in his *Memoir of the Future*.

An endoskeletonal personality (Bion) evolves from within, is not imposed from outside in the form of codes of behaviour. Coleridge in *Biographia Literaria* called this activation of the spirit of growth in poetry 'ab intra' (organically) not 'superinduced', 'ab extra' (mechanically). As Bion said, if it is hard to read poetry, how equally hard it must be to read people. He often spoke of the third person in the room, the internal observer or observers of both patient and analyst. Meltzer however was much clearer than Bion in insisting that the analysis is being conducted by his objects in communion with the internal objects of the patient. Without this psychoanalysis would still be twodimensional, a sign-language, a 'talking about' rather than a 'becoming' through symbol formation. Meltzer said that symbol formation was indeed the key to unlocking two-dimensionality and the aesthetic dilemma of autistic defences.[27] For this, psychoanalysis has to be a present experience; so Bion's emphasis on eschewing memory and desire provided a missing link which was necessary before Meltzer could elucidate the function of 'beauty' in clinical psychoanalysis, through the concept of the aesthetic conflict. This, in turn, enables a new structural link between psychoanalysis and art forms such as literature, which has as yet only begun to be developed.

An example: Keats

Keats, in his great Odes, demonstrated the impossibility of fusion – of being mystically swallowed up by the object, to 'cease upon the midnight with no pain'; yet this did not mean death in the sense of abandonment by the symbol-making gods; the nightingale may sing in the next valley-glade. This is the last stanza of his 'Ode to a Nightingale':

> Forlorn! the very word is like a bell
>> To toll me back from thee to my sole self!
> Adieu! the fancy cannot cheat so well
>> As she is fam'd to do, deceiving elf.
> Adieu! adieu! thy plaintive anthem fades
>> Past the near meadows, over the still stream,
>>> Up the hill-side; and now 'tis buried deep
>>> In the next valley-glades
>> Was it a vision, or a waking dream?
>>> Fled is that music:—Do I wake or sleep?[28]

In a series of 'adieus', the poet longingly traces the bird's fading song through the everyday landscape, including a gentle, wistful rebuke that the fancy has *not* cheated him – has not allowed him to fade away into the forest dim, to cease upon the midnight with no pain. He has to come to terms with the fact not that the experience was an illusion, but that he is alone once more: that not he, but the Nightingale, is fading away. The burial-place which he gives the song in his imagination, however, 'deep/ In the next valley glades', is not a purely natural habitat, but recalls the sensuous enclosure of the aching heart with which the poem began, and the embalmed darkness at the centre of the experience. When the song is no longer audible, its underground rhythm still pulses; the Nightingale still exists and is remembered. The ache of a 'happiness' which at the beginning of the poem threatened to lead to Lethe has instead found a place in the Vale of Soul-making.

And finally, the last two lines of the poem look at the experience from the outside, framing it, giving context to the psychic drama that up to now has been viewed subjectively: was it a vision or a waking dream? asks the poet. He conveys both the mystical moment of knowledge and the sense of disorientation that arises as a result of conversing with the object. There is a further process of digestion to take place. No reverie, no thought-process, is ever finished: each episode merely opens up the next stage in the mind's journey, following the Nightingale into the next valley-glade. The song, or mental feed, is no longer heard but neither is it lost, since the listening self (the baby) has an increased capacity for imaginative introjection.

Conclusion

So psychoanalysis as an art form depends absolutely on an appreciation of the analysis as an aesthetic object, and of the psychoanalytic method as a beautiful means of revealing the influence of the object – one might almost say (as do the poets with their Muse), paying homage to the object, as in Keats's lines to Psyche:

> Yes, I will be thy priest, and build a fane
> In some untrodden region of my mind,
> Where branched thoughts, new grown with pleasant pain,
> Instead of pines shall murmur in the wind:[29]

The underlying idea in both poetry and psychoanalysis is, of course, that of individual development: to rely on the internalised teaching object rather than on projective identification with a narcissistic substitute, and in this way, to become oneself rather than a pale shadow of somebody else.

Meltzer says he was 'impressed by the experience of the beauty of the process which regularly emerges' during the weaning phase of an analysis, and which he realised was also present in his patients at that stage. The sense of beauty was a sign of the threshold of the depressive position, the point at which an analysis could come to a natural end since its thinking processes were internalisable.

It is an indication that a complex form of introjection is taking place in which the thinking function (alpha function) of the analyst's mind is becoming part of the patient's own equipment. It is useful if the patient can understand the analyst's thoughts about him, on the discursive level of sign-systems. This is part of the scientific body of knowledge that he is accumulating. But it is far more essential that the patient introject the analyst's *capacity to think* about him, on the level of symbol-formation, if he is to be able to continue the process of self-analysis which is the ultimate goal of the psychoanalytic art. What is hoped for is not just to establish dependence on the introjected object, but to acquire through inspiration its capacity for clear sight and responsibility.

> Thus an adult appreciation of the beauty and goodness of the analytic process and method of discovering the truth can begin to sort itself out from the infantile transference which seems to attach itself so tenaciously to the person of the analyst. He can now be seen to preside over the process in a way which reasonably yields to the assumption of these responsibilities by the patient himself.[30]

And this happens in the context of recognising that the analysis itself is the aesthetic object, the ultimate product of its aesthetic method.

This elaborates a new definition of analytic 'success' which distinguishes it from social adaptability, normality, or relief from symptoms, that analysts these days consider unsatisfactory. In this sense the analytic process is itself the artwork, capable of going beyond the experience of one analytic couple and being employed in an increasingly sophisticated way by future couples – the future babies of psychoanalysis, or 'hungry generations' in Keats's words.

Donald Meltzer used to refer to psychoanalysis as 'conversations between internal objects', and this is how I saw my working relationship with him, bringing in the role of the poets as internal objects for the psychoanalytic process. Meltzer also adopted occasionally the Kantian phrase that Bion often used, about psychoanalysis as 'a thing-in-itself' – meaning a spirit underlying not just official art forms but all types of humanistic endeavour. Psychoanalysis, in Meltzer's view of Bion, is an idea that has always existed, but it had to be 'thought', it had to get into the world – beginning with the 'mystic genius' of Freud but then spreading outwards, following (as the Milton said) 'the idea of beauty through all the shapes and forms of things'. Or as Virginia Woolf expresses it: 'It is not exactly beauty that I mean. It is that the thing is in itself enough: satisfactory; achieved'.[31]

This Platonic underlying idea, which is essentially that of psychic development, is engaged in some way by all creative writers or artists, and Meltzer saw psychoanalysis as finally acknowledging its antecedents and joining the 'family' of the artists in the communal search for psychic reality.[32] In the words of Virginia Woolf, who imagined there was a 'pattern' of reality behind the 'cotton wool' of appearances, that we experience in moments of turbulence: 'Behind the cotton wool is hidden a pattern, that the whole world is a work of art; we are parts of it … We are the words, we are the music, we are the thing itself'.[33]

Notes

1 This paper was originally presented as a talk at the anniversary celebration for Donald Meltzer given in Buenos Aires, 19–20 August 2022.

2 *The Apprehension of Beauty: The Role of Aesthetic Conflict in Development, Art, and Violence*. New edition: London: Harris Meltzer Trust, 2018, p. 215.

3 *Studies in Extended Metapsychology*. New edition: London: Harris Meltzer Trust, 2018, p. 87.

4 See M. H. Williams, 'Could Beauty help? Responses to turbulence' http://www.artlit.info/pdfs/CouldBeautyHelp.pdf

5 R. J. Harris, *Selected Poems*. Perthshire: Clunie Press, 1970. https://www.harris-meltzer-trust.org.uk/pdfs/HarrisPoems1970.pdf

6 S. Langer, *Philosophy in a New Key: A Study in the Symbolism of Reason, Rite and Art*. Harvard University Press, 1941.

7 M. H. Williams, 'Holding the dream: the nature of aesthetic appreciation', in *The Apprehension of Beauty*. New edition: London: Harris Meltzer Trust, 2018, p. 187.

8 See on YouTube: https://youtu.be/_wQNA3JkiyI and https://youtu.be/14Wc8U6m2_w

9 Meltzer, jacket cover to D. Meltzer & M. H. Williams, *The Apprehension of Beauty*. Original edition: Perthshire: Clunie Press, 1988.

10 Meltzer, jacket cover to M. H. Williams, *Inspiration in Milton and Keats*. Basingstoke: Macmillan, 1982.

11 Meltzer, Foreword to M. H. Williams, *The Vale of Soulmaking: The Post-Kleinian Model of the Mind*. London: Karnac, 2005, pp. xix, xii.

12 M. H. Williams, 'Macbeth's equivocation: Shakespeare's ambiguity', in D. Meltzer, *The Claustrum*. Perthshire: Clunie Press, 1991.

13 Emily Dickinson, 'I dwell in Possibility'. First published 1929. https://en.wikisource.org/wiki/I_dwell_in_Possibility_— Creative Commons Attribution-ShareAlike license.

14 *Dream Life: A Re-examination of the Psychoanalytical Theory and Technique*. New edition: London: Harris Meltzer Trust, 2018, p. 165.

15 *Dream Life: A Re-examination of the Psychoanalytical Theory and Technique*. New edition: London: Harris Meltzer Trust, 2018, p. 151.

16 Meltzer, 'On thought disorders'. In: *Selected Papers of Donald Meltzer*, vol. 2. London: Harris Meltzer Trust, 2021, p. 82.

17 Romana Negri, introduction to R. Negri & M. Harris, *The Story of Infant Development: Observational Work with Martha Harris*. London: Harris Meltzer Trust, 2007, p. xviii.

18 Meltzer, 'Bion's Grid'. In: *Selected Papers of Donald Meltzer*, vol. 2. London: Harris Meltzer Trust, 2021, p. 111.

19 A. Stokes, *Painting and the Inner World*, extracts in: *Art and Analysis: An Adrian Stokes Reader*, ed. M. H. Williams. London: Harris Meltzer Trust, 2014, p. 124.

20 Bion, *A Memoir of the Future*, vol. 2.

21 'On thought disorders'. In: *Selected Papers of Donald Meltzer*, vol. 2, p. 74. London: Harris Meltzer Trust, 2021.

22 'Temperature and distance as technical dimensions of interpretation'. In: *Selected Papers of Donald Meltzer* vol. 3. London: Harris Meltzer Trust, 2021.

23 *Studies in Extended Metapsychology*, p. 250.

24 'On supervision'. Meltzer with R. and M. Oelsner. In: *Selected Papers of Donald Meltzer*, vol. 3. London: Harris Meltzer Trust, 2021, p. 20.

25 Keats, 'Ode on a Grecian Urn'.

26 W. R. Bion, *Attention and Interpretation*. London: Tavistock, 1970.

27 *Studies in Extended Metapsychology*, p. 247.

28 https://www.poetryfoundation.org/poems/44479/ode-to-a-nightingale

29 'Ode to Psyche': https://www.poetryfoundation.org/poems/44480/ode-to-psyche

30 *The Psychoanalytical Process*. (1967). New edition: London: Harris Meltzer Trust, 2018, p. 48.

31 V. Woolf, Diary of 1926, *A Writer's Diary*, ed. L. Woolf. New York: Harcourt, 1954, p. 85.

32 Meltzer, Foreword to M. H. Williams, *The Vale of Soulmaking*, p. xix.

33 V. Woolf, 'Sketch of the Past'. In: *Moments of Being*, ed. J. Schulkind and H. Lee. London: Pimlico, 2002, p. 83.

2 Grievance, change and the phantasy of perfect knowledge

Abbot A. Bronstein, PhD

Introduction

My history with Donald Meltzer as a child, adult and eventually a psychoanalyst were significant influences in my life. The first book he gave to me, around age 10, was C.S. Lewis' **The Magician's Nephew**. I had not understood as a child what a magician Don was. He was simply my uncle who had moved to London with all my cousins. The relationship and centrality of his presence in my life and my family's life continued from my birth until his death.

Don was a significant and towering figure in psychoanalysis. His originality and clinical brilliance, as a teacher, writer and supervisor were obvious to any who would hear or read his ideas. My first experience of him as a psychoanalyst and not merely my uncle was at a talk he gave at the William Alanson White Institute in the early 1970s. The paper and clinical discussion was memorable. It was entitled "Timing and Tact in Psychoanalysis". His thesis was that analytic process and interpretation to bring about change are not governed by timing and tact, but by 'truth'. Meltzer's major interest was the psychoanalytic process: the creation of a setting within which this complex process could occur.

His clinical case discussion was extraordinary. He had a unique capacity to weave a creative story about the internal world and life of a person as well as to articulate ideas related to unconscious phantasy and the internal movement of objects within a lively clinical discussion. For me it had only been on paper, words in a book previously.

Clinical paper: the case of Ms. A

Ms. A lived in a psychic world of completeness unto herself, joined together with her own body and mind, an omnipotent and omniscience phantasy was part of this complete sense of herself. Psychically, she was in a perfect union with her analyst. It was not a union where change was possible nor truly needed.

DOI: 10.4324/9781003441861-3

The terror involved in change and the courage to take part in the process of analysis where change might occur are needed by both participants in the psychoanalytic endeavor.

In this paper, I address intertwined and inter-related topics. The first topic is the experience of grievance itself. The second is the way in which grievances are 'nursed' (Feldman, 2008). Feldman describes the consequent resentments that hold the patient and analyst from analytic movement and from achieving psychic change – in essence, from grieving itself. The third point I will make is how these two previous issues, at times, encompass a vibrant yet stultifying, deadening unconscious phantasy of perfection and completeness. In such cases, patient and analyst have the impression that there is little need or interest for new knowledge as knowing has already been attained.

I will first address some theoretical issues before moving to the clinical case of Ms. A.

Mrs. A's quest for perfect knowledge included the perfect union of both minds and bodies. The perfect couple existed within the unconscious phantasy. The union had already been obtained, so that any alterations in this internal world implied an unacceptable sacrifice that she and other patients only approach with great caution, fear and distrust.

There are patients[1] who seem to regularly respond with either an attitude or a direct statement of "I know that already!" Whatever the analyst proposes, they appear to omnisciently know already about themselves and their internal worlds. They believe they have knowledge without having obtained it from the analytic process or help of their analyst. They dream, explore, interpret and 'know' they understand themselves, but remain analytically or psychically unchanged by this knowledge. There is little to no insight that can bring real change. The so-called knowledge they possess creates a difficulty within the treatment where analytic work and knowledge challenges their so-called knowledge, where psychic truth disrupts their internal stability.

The patients I am attempting to describe in this paper cut across diagnostic categories. They have in common the extraordinary and persistent attachment to their grievances and to their conviction about the truth about events in their past. The complaints about their 'objects' are very different from what Freud referred to as 'suffering from reminiscences' that Freud described. The psychic configuration of these patients is such that they experience great psychic pain, despair, and envy while seeking revenge that as a consequence makes others suffer along with them. As analysts, we are exposed to a narrative of the past that appears at times to have been unbearably cruel while simultaneously being exposed to being treated with contempt, mocking and derision. The analyst is blamed for causing their suffering, and for withholding the knowledge that would relieve them from that repeated experience. In the transference, the analyst becomes yet another object who is unable or unwilling to help (Segal,

1994; Feldman, 2008). The analyst begins to feel that they never seem to be able to truly understand the pain and cruelty experienced as a result of the experience of having been expelled from the Garden of Eden (Steiner, 2018). The analyst must struggle and tolerate the bearing of the intense discomfort associated with becoming another of these cruel objects. They must come to realize that by not allowing change, they perpetuate the 'unbearable' past to which the patient seems so deeply wedded.

Isaiah Berlin, the British philosopher (2000) attempted to describe both a unifying idea of truth that mankind strives to achieve and that "of the perfect society, wholly just" that is only interfered with by others. The patient I will describe lives by this edict. They live in a world in which others interfere with their finding perfection. They are perfect unto themselves.

In the patients I am describing, one can identify the centrality of the real or imagined knowledge of the primal scene and an anal masturbatory ritual that falsely gives understanding and knowledge. In this manner, change would not be a consequence of the work of analysis; instead it would occur via a different process. In A's words it was "as if there's some magic door, I need to go through in order to change!"[2] The relationship of this to reverie, the aesthetic object and the combined object will be touched upon briefly. These interconnected phantasies were central to Donald Meltzer's conception of the analytic process and the way in which change might occur. The door, like that in C.S. Lewis' the Magician's Nephew however, is inevitably the wrong door for these people. The search for perfect knowledge is more an effort *to prove that one already has obtained that knowledge*. The analysis is the danger as it attempts to describe and show the patient how such so-called knowledge traps them in a world where nothing changes.

For Freud, witnessing or knowledge related to the sexual relationship of the parents brought about increases in sexual excitement that was transformed into anxiety due to the inability to 'understand' and cope with the experience. Trauma is understood when the system conscious, such as described by Freud, overwhelms the person's psyche. Developing a character trait that conveys certainty and conviction about knowing becomes a way to protect from the anxiety of not knowing, of not understanding. This is in clear opposition to the analytic wish to provide a useful mind, a place where constructive, generative thought is possible seeking truths that are emotional nutrients. Here that 'wish' is thwarted.

The mind seeks truth as a nutrient. This search takes place in the realm where "beauty is truth, truth is beauty". For the patients I'm describing, this analytic 'wish' is thwarted and confounded by the worship of a false world of truths, in which truth is perverted: where the inevitable pain of real knowing, understanding and thinking is replaced by the magical omnipotent false world (Segal, 2006). The path these patients take to search for the 'truth' is through a magical world which at times can have a delusional quality, making it difficult for them to stay in touch with reality.

Uncertainty and doubt is not a welcome goal. These patients are terrified of experiencing differences, recognizing that one is separated from the other who have their own thoughts. The analytic work aiming at dealing with this terror and at recognizing the falseness of the unions the patient has created, leads to firestorms of protest, rage, outbursts and attacks on the analyst internally and externally. A creative combined object where genuine intercourse exists and thinking is permitted is assiduously avoided.

In the work with these patients, the analyst must be wary of the shifts between what seems to be part of a genuine unique analytic couple that produces new ideas and an idealized couple that worships false insight. These patients feel so grievously harmed by others, that they hold onto the grievances and thwart and prevent change in the internal world. In this state the phantasy of a combined object, an object that is all things, needing no other is developed and maintained. Intercourse is not sought with others except to fulfill the phantasy that the other is not needed, the other one is oneself.

There is a great deal of literature written already about patients such as these from varying vantage points. Betty Joseph (1985, 1992) has described the 'chuntering' and perverse pleasure such patients manifest in the analysis. John Steiner (1996) in his paper on "Revenge and Resentment" has described the vengeful nature of their interactions and the constant accusations which act as psychic retreats. Steiner explores in detail the way in which the act of forgiveness is difficult to achieve in the face of the grievances preventing psychic change. Lucy LaFarge (2006) has written on the topic of revenge as well speaking to some of the same points as Steiner. Elizabeth Spillius (1993) in her paper on "Varieties of Envious Experiences" speaks to something similar in her descriptions of 'impenitent' envy: envy that is felt to be justified by the person, giving rise to virulent hatred. Lansky (1994) has written about the shame and humiliation and the state of unforgiveness such patients suffer and the way in which they vividly communicate these states to the analyst during the analysis. Ron Britton et al. (1989) and Michael Feldman (1989) have written about the analyst's and patient's capacity to be creative or to act as a creative couple is disrupted by the patient's sadistic attacks. Feldman's description of the attack on the internal parental couple and Segal's description of 'freedom of thought' are in some way close to the clinical situation I am describing in this paper.

The subject of grievance, hurt, suffering and vengeance is explored in novels, plays and movies. The persecutory hatred that fills the object who is abused, and the acts of vengeance directed toward those that are considered the cause of the hurt, capture our attention and hold us riveted.[3]

There is an etymological-linguistic link between the concepts of grievance, grieving and grief. The link points us toward a possible connection between three concepts: that of causing grievous harm, doing an injustice resulting in pain. In other words, the link between an act that causes

pain: "to cause to be sorrowful" and that of the act of grieving. [4] Grievances burden the mind, oppress and bring hardship to oneself. To feel
grief, means to feel sorrow and sadness. Grieving, the act of mourning
the loss of a relationship, internal or external, is thwarted by maintaining
the grievance against those internal and external objects that caused the
pain. Grievances don't easily become transformed into grief through the
process of grieving, this transformation would require a shift from feeling
persecuted by one's world, to one where change can take place.

The detailed clinical example is from one of the longest analyses conducted in my analytic career. I came to realize that my perseverance and
that of the patient was in part an enactment, to find perfection within the
clinical work. In this manner, the threat to change was enacted by the
analyst as well.

Psychoanalysis puts forward the hypothesis that it is in part through
the 'emotional storms', as portrayed by Strachey (1934) in his descriptions
of mutative interpretations, and as Bion later describes, that we create the
atmosphere in the analysis within which psychic change occurs. These
storms are particularly intense with aggrieved patients, as one is drawn
into both gross and subtle transference and countertransference enact-
ments. The emergence into a newly populated external and internal universe is extraordinarily slow and painful for them. There is the risk of
these analyses becoming interminable analyses if one can't manage one's
own disappointment of ending without perfection being achieved. The
patients who suffer from such pervasive and persistent grievances **will
not** permit the past to **not** be the present. This is, I believe, what Feldman
(2008) describes in his notion of the nursing of grievances. One can think
that they hold themselves, the analysis and the analyst hostage to a past
that prevents genuine psychic change.

At the start of analysis, the idea of change is something which Ms. A
seemed to desire very openly. She was very agreeable and had great hope
for the process itself. The analyst also felt this hope and desire and despite
the fact that other treatments had failed, he offers analyses. The shared
belief of analyst and patient might be summarized as 'This analysis will
be different, the patient is at a different point in her lives, more motivated
to alter what has become a stalemate in their lives or their previous treatments. They are not resistant to change – they desperately, consciously
and overtly wish to change — and we will be the agent of that change'.

It is as if the analyst identifies with the patient and the grievances she expresses against previous analysts and the world itself. One becomes an ally,
without awareness, against the promise of analysis and psychic change.

Ms. A

A had been in analysis for over a decade. A decision was made to stop
meeting. There had been numerous other attempts at ending, but none
had 'succeeded'. Ms. A was now in her late 60's.

She was married twice for very brief times, she had one daughter who was in her 40's, who was married and has two small children.

Ms. A was born in Romania. At the time of the rise of National Socialism, her family moved to Egypt and then to Israel. When she was an adolescent she moved to French speaking Canada. The family went from wealthy aristocratic – French speaking – to poverty numerous times in her childhood. This painful and repetitive ascent and descent in status was a primary 'trauma' for her family. English was her 4th language, but one she spoke fluently. Highly educated, competent and very interesting, she was a survivor as were her parents, in a most literal sense – but they were **'survivors with pretensions'** as she once described.

Her mother was the most important person ostensibly, with servants caring for her and the father being kept somewhat apart from direct caretaking, as the story was told. He was ordered to wear white sanitary gloves when holding her. Mostly she was handed to the mother at certain times and interactions, such as feeding and bedtime. This narrative seemed less and less accurate as time went on, but it remained as a central theme: she was cared for by others and not by the ones who should want to care for her.

A's had an overriding sense of being excluded, literally shut out, from others lives. She told and retold the story of being excluded from the parents bedroom when she was 6, banished and condemned to share a room with her grandmother. "They were poor, it was a financial uncertainty. There were not enough bedrooms". Though actually cared for by her grandmother, the description was that they were both excluded from the important places in the house. In her mind, this was at the source of the main grievance that explained her life to her.

Shortly after being 'banished' from the parents bedroom, Ms. A began a secret anal masturbatory ritual[5] of inserting items that belonged to her mother into her anus, looking in the mirror and being very pleased. The anal masturbatory ritual continued over years into adult masturbatory behaviors moving to the clitoris and vagina. She would use foods, which maintained the anal, fecal aspects of the masturbatory unconscious phantasy. As a small child, she was excited by the masturbatory experiences, she was very pleased with the excitement she was able to produce by herself, including the secret wrongness of the act. I thought that through the masturbatory activities, she had found a way of putting things together, in phantasy, becoming and being both parts of the parental couple and maternal/baby couple and no longer needing the other at all.

The masturbatory activities and phantasies were not used as a transitional object, but a perverse one. Objects weren't replaced temporarily to fix a sense of loss or aloneness. What A found was, in a sense better, it was under her complete omnipotent control. Being left out was still the grievance but she had found a way to not need to be included any longer. With things in her life being so 'imperfect' she had managed to maintain a perfect bond with herself and internal objects. This was my organizing speculation to myself early in the analysis which helped me create an illusion of having some understanding. Her pain associated with the lack of connection with her mother was resolved through perverse action. But it is important to stress that I was joining with her in this quest to make an illusion a reality.

An important memory with her mother: between 6 and 9 years of age, while living in a place where there was intense military activity with raids, bombing and hiding places, A would create stories for her mother when she would come home from school. Her father was also frequently away on secret military activities during this time. These fantastic stories were to entertain her mother – *"making beauty out of ugliness"*, in her words.

Two important memories are worth mentioning. They were told with little affect when reported. The first one was about her mother constantly complaining about the father's extra marital interests, bitterly feeling she would never be able to go back to the life of wealth and prestige she left behind in Europe. The second was about a sibling, a baby boy that was born before Ms. A who was "damaged" and died. This was never spoken about. Ms. A told these memories with little affect. The facts around the birth and death remained a mystery. Ms. A never understood if the birth defects her dead sibling suffered from were life threatening or if the baby's life was ended because he was not 'perfect'. The phantasy of being perfect being threatened with death if that was not realized, remained throughout her life.

I will now discuss a first session about 10 years into the analysis where she brought up again her wish to stop the analysis. A began with a complaint about another "inadequate man who doesn't measure up". She "knows" this is a common theme we have talked about endlessly in the analysis. When she mentioned this being aware that the analyst knows she is once again repeating this, Ms. A is subtly mocking of the analyst and of the familiar but useless interpretations that he has made regarding these repetitions. She proceeds to describe in detail how this man is disrespectful of her, her daughter and the woman with whom he lives. She describes him as being scruffy, not Jewish, arrogant and condescending. She then interprets for herself. She imagines she has behaved this way because of the weekend break. She links it to the fact that she had brought up ending the analysis last week. She believes she has to give herself a reason for not quitting the analysis. She feels this clearly explains her behavior toward this man at the party.

My impression and reaction was that A was not truly curious about her behavior. Instead she was performing for my benefit. This was a typical exchange in the analysis where some possible interesting behavior was quickly dismissed by her giving it an old meaning in a rather lifeless fashion. I attempted to point out to her how she bypassed the need for any input from me, her analyst with something we both already knew.

A. then proceeded quickly to tell me a dream: "it has something to do with a man who killed somebody or thinks he did and he's trying to find out. He's crouching or hiding behind a fence and his friends, and I'm one of them, we are trying to say you don't need to look – you need to come away from this". A. continued, without pause, to talk about how she had made her daughter and granddaughter uncomfortable over the weekend by getting angry toward the man she met at the party.

She rushed on talking about the party over the weekend showing no interest in thinking about the dream, but simply continued, once again, expressing her grievance against this man.

Ms. A appeared to be inviting the analyst to intervene. She did this by talking about her feeling that she has not been a very good patient, by her lack of associations to the dream, or by continuing to complain about one thing or another. I thought we were in a familiar loop. I would say what I was expected to say and she would hear nothing new. It would be lifeless.

I tried, in a somewhat faltering way, to point out this expectation. She then, I felt, compliantly talked a little about the dream; how "the man was searching behind the fence and I was trying to dissuade him from finding something out – like the truth". She then added with emotion, that she just wanted to kill that man at the party.

I was quite unaware of the once again enactment: that is, going back and forth stating our 'thoughtful' and 'known' observations. This left me very unsettled and frustrated, in a way as she felt with this man at the party. But, I pushed further not realizing the fact that I had already been defeated and felt quite despairing of my useless way of working.

I suggested that the manner in which she was talking was intended to keep something hidden – that we were to believe that we were really looking for something here today in the analysis – that we were supposedly looking together for the truth. We could see how I was being led to find out only what was already in plain sight. I was to be dissuaded from looking for a new discovery, thinking about what had happened over the weekend, or even about a genuine discussion of the topic of stopping the analysis at some point.

A. immediately began to talk about her railing against this man, she had more complaints about him, and she said that she knew that this was always what she did. This continued for a few minutes.

In retrospect I think we might see here how the analyst is drawn into talking about analysis ending, yet being told by the patient what he already knows and is known to the patient. The analyst becomes someone who the patient can rail against, but who also, in a frustrated despairing state, rails against the patient, complaining that she is not doing her job as a patient. The man is not the 'right' man, crude, not Jewish, not knowing how to behave at such an event. He is anything but perfect. The analyst is looking for the perfect interpretation but through sleight of hand, mis-directed and becomes a rather useless, repetitive object, while stuck in the mutual phantasy that together they will find answers.

During the session, there weren't new thoughts or associations – we both remained racing about – running in place from idea to idea – but the real crime or if there even is a crime stays hidden from the analyst and the analysis.

What I want to stress is not whether or not my interpretations were correct. What I want to stress instead is the fact that A sets up a situation in which neither the analyst nor the patient can stay in emotionally alive contact for very long. We are working together but in parallel to each other. Like what happens in parallel play in children: interacting but not building something together, we are struggling to be an analytic generative couple.

Interpretation that makes emotional contact brings about both some resolution of anxiety, as well as the heightening of the precipice we walk between the old and the new. Thus there is always an element of awareness of a depressive response (Applegarth, personal communication). Contact with something new, such as a new idea either in the analyst's mind or the patient's, fosters separateness, creates disruption (Caper, 1997). Emotional aliveness pushes the patient and analyst toward anxiety, a depressive anxiety, showing the patient something of the process of grief and mourning that must take place for psychic change to occur.

With Ms. A the value of the interpretations was not because they provide knowledge or demonstrate a capacity of thinking. The value came from the ability of Ms. A to stop the analyst from functioning as a partner/analyst – as someone who can really help her shift her internal world. Rather, A becomes compliant, somewhat false and the analyst becomes frustrated, a bit insistent of his 'overvalued' ideas expressed in the form of interpretations. This becomes a not so subtle sado-masochistic enactment that stops the genuine satisfying and pleasurable intercourse of the analytic situation. Our joining isn't generative but repetitive of a very old somewhat dysfunctional internal couple where there is little room to think creatively.

My impression when this happened, is that A's past was brought into the transference and countertransference in the consulting room; she is experiencing an exciting but non-creative masturbatory interaction with the analyst. In some fashion she recreates the false, looking in the mirror, anal masturbatory activity that makes her both parts of the couple in the intercourse. The patient is embroiled in her 'grievance' against this man, but the analyst is outside of this, he is the man to whom she comes with her confession. So the analyst and patient recreate a kind of interaction that combines the couple not as a creative pair in real intercourse, or creative combined object producing something new, but as a false couple, that stops the creative process of thinking.

This creates a situation where neither she nor I will not have to face the anxiety and despair of our truly thinking about ending the analysis, whether it is or is not the time to end. In this manner, we can remain a falsely idealized couple, with a perfect false melding of what we are each thinking. She knows my mind, what she believes I wish to hear, and I tell her what she already knows. Thus, we can go on for a very long time – an interminable amount of time, staying aligned against others but not aligned as analyst and patient for the purpose of new discovery.

Some months later she comes to the session and brings a dream. "I am on a deck. You are there with another woman and I am behind you and you don't quite see me. I want to be with you but there is no room, no place in-between you and her. There is a place on the other side of you, but I don't want to be there. I don't want to be on the other side. You then speak to me, but I am not happy. I then go off to the bathroom or something".

At this point, we were now no longer focused on her ending the analysis. She seemed re-engaged in the work while also holding fast to knowing and assuring herself that analysis would eventually provide her with a somewhat magical solution to her loneliness and despair.

However, during this period, there was a somewhat more realistic view that she (as the dream expresses), is the child in the couple and that she is sharing the mother/father/analyst with others. She is unhappy with her place outside the couple and retreats into the bathroom-bottom anal masturbatory activity, which absorbs her interest and protects against the overwhelming psychic pain of being excluded. But, I thought there was some evidence that she was struggling, and that the bathroom/masturbatory solution was no longer as effective.

Yet, she would still blame her analyst/mother for not choosing her over the man on the deck of the boat. Once again she retreated into the usual associations that we had heard so many times previously.

When she brought new material, my hope that it would be something new was wiped away by the associations that were very familiar. They were both attempts to be compliant and reasonable. But they stymied the sense of something new that the analyst hoped was appearing.

My desire for newness and change was thwarted by both my wishes for something new and by her continually stalemating the situation with what she knew things meant. There were cracks in this armor, but small ones.

I attempted to show and interpret to A that the dream seemed to indicate that I wasn't interested enough in her to include her in the way she wished; that she was being given a space but it was not the in-between space – the right space in my mind and life. The analyst is both the paternal figure who can be abusive and the maternal figure who cannot survive without. But, there is a flaw in this idea, in as much as there is a space being made for her – just not the space that she insists she must have. So she goes off again into the world of self-sufficiency, eliminating the sense of being excluded. But she was actually invited to join.

I thought she had moved for a moment, toward a more genuine sense of emotionally alive contact. My intervention was about the dream, including that she had felt unsettled for a moment when she realized that the space she wanted did not match what I offered her in my mind and in my thoughts. What happened in regards to this intervention was unclear. Perhaps Ms. A wished that there was nobody else in that space that could come between us.

We both knew the facts of her history all too well. They are screen memories in her mind, but also mine. Her goal has been to appear as if she wants to search for the discovery of a new fact that would explain things differently to both of us. But this keeps us both stuck with a repetition that had little analytic effect. What I was slowly beginning to comprehend was the *terror* she felt at anything being changed, at anything new and different and unknown that needed to be understood by both of us.

Unlike some of my other more disturbed and pervasively stuck patients, A. knows something about herself – she is despairing and desperate, but largely unable to see the way in which she affects others negatively. The reason why things remain sterile is more subtle than I could articulate. My impression is that Ms. A has interest in my interpretations and it looks as if we are working together. However, the reality is that we are not 'combined' in a fashion that allows us to produce something new between. This gives me the feeling that I am stuck and impoverished in my interpretations and my understanding. I keep on repeating to myself to keep hope alive, that new results will be possible.

Uncharacteristically, after the session I just described, A said: "I feel like I'm torturing you, I feel like I'm stale". This made me feel a bit more hopeful, that perhaps she no longer had to be the perfect idealized patient with an overly idealized analyst. The mood in the analysis slowly shifted, I then began to feel a more genuine interest in her more sympathy and a more alive hope. I began to feel I was allowed to experience some pleasure in being useful – as long as I didn't become too excited with the feeling that I was always being a helpful analyst.

Psychic change involves the patient developing real concern for others, as opposed to some useful behavioral changes that will not be meaningful after the analysis ends.

About a year passed and we were seriously considering ending this long analysis. At times, Ms. A seemed to become genuinely disturbed by her lack of change and my inability to help her. We were increasingly a somewhat failed analyst-patient couple, disappointing each other, looking stupid, incompetent, disliking each other much of the time.

As we were closer to ending, she had a frightening dream. "I was in an airplane and they are trying to land on a roadway and cars are coming from the opposite direction and the plane is veering left and right to try to land on this roadway—it was pretty dangerous". This dream expressed A's sense of herself as "complete", with all the parts needed for the omnipotent manic phantasy of self-sufficiency started to break down somehow. Moreover, the dream also communicated that the pilot/analyst was not doing a very good job in bringing the flight/analysis.

A few days later, Ms. A brought another dream: "there were dozens of pastries, she had taken one of each kind even though this was forbidden". In her desire to take one of everything that she also knows is forbidden, she appears to be struggling with her envious of "being an aristocrat, a noble person" not one of the commoners who feel envy. Her sense of distress and despair at ever being able to change became increasingly a part of the analytic work. For Ms. A the analysis became more unpleasant and disturbing, for the analyst, it felt more "real", more hopeful that the analysis could eventually end. She began to express subtle and direct negative feelings toward the analyst: the phantasy that he was off with his wife on a vacation dressed in clown pants, demeaned, foolish and the object of derision. Others have been victim to such views, but the analyst had previously always lived in a protected fortress, with her, against those objects, not one of them.

The end of analysis had become a real possibility, it seemed. She could recognize with pain its limitations.

After her return from holidays, A. canceled her first session. After a number of successive phone calls she finally decided that she can actually make the session. In the session, she tells a dream about a workman who wanted to make love, but since it is the first date, this would not be a change of the rules. A thinks that her dream is related to her having come back from holidays to the analysis, she thinks it is time to set up a termination date. During this period A. becomes increasingly upset when I interpret she may be anxious about her return to the analysis. She says this intervention does not resonate with her, she feels that I am actually tormenting her. It is so difficult for her to tolerate that we are not always in harmony.

I had used the word anxiety about coming to session and starting back in the analysis. She objected saying she doesn't understand why I am using that word when she isn't anxious. She doesn't understand and is quite upset that I used such a word. It isn't what she was thinking at all.

Ms. A doesn't like, at all, that she and I are not on the same page, not of one mind, not joined in a state of mutual understanding about what the analytic couple are thinking. We are different from before. She can't finish my sentences. This has become increasingly troublesome and she doesn't know why I insist on 'tormenting' her in this way. What is my purpose!

In the session, A. continues being very upset. She thinks about having called about not coming, and then changes her mind. She wanted to make up the session and not have to pay for not getting something. She has always hated having to pay for sessions she can't attend!

She thinks about a man who for 50 years has wanted to sleep with her, but she doesn't feel that way about him. He is just sort of a friend, but not a very good one.

From what I could understand, I commented that something had been taken away from her by me during the break. She wanted it back to make things whole again. She resents that I have something that makes me whole and she doesn't. I suggested that she felt I torment her because my interventions make her feel that, without the analysis, she feels incomplete and imperfect and she recognizes her need and dependency. This makes her vulnerable to loss. She struggles with the intimacy associated with the analysis. She reacts very upset to this interventions and she leaves the session. In many ways, I had looked forward to this breach for a long time.

Ms. A, after a long analysis, always waiting for the perfect moment to stop, had set a date for ending with the analyst concurring. It would not change as it had done before. Being a very 'good' patient was quite important and having a *very good* analysis with me, even more so.

The patient brought one last dream very near the end of the analysis: "there is a dog sitting on my (Ms. A's) lap, but I don't see the dog, I see a banana. The dog's head has been cut off but the dog is alive as a banana and is moving. But it has no head! "She says that the dreams make no sense. After a while, she says and she can't remember anything else about it. Then quickly she adds "I think I'm emasculating you so I can justify my ending (the analysis)". It's what comes to mind! She said emphatically. "I know it's not an association".

In the dream, one can see that she brings us back to the combined object as well as the history of masturbation with fruit, which had been part of the analysis earlier on. I intervened, telling her that she knew I was going to speak about her envy, and even her penis envy (the dog as a banana with its head cut off). There is the envy of the way my mind works. Can I be put to use by working with her? She needs my mind to work and hers to work too, even if we are connected in the analysis any longer. What will she do when the analysis ends?

Her response to this intervention was that she did not feel it was necessary to associate, she already knew what I was going to say. This meant for her that I had no mind left, if she were to associate it would be for my benefit, in this way it was my own envy that was at play, perhaps I would like to steal back his mind or seek revenge for what she has taken.

One can think that her reaction to my intervention implied that she now had my mind as her own on her lap so to speak. In this way, she could now end the analysis because she had what she needed the most from me – my mind in perfect union with hers. Can I allow her to now leave me out of the combined parental bedroom where she can think on her own? Can she change in an imperfect manner and feel that would be enough?

Can I allow her and the analysis, the change, the interpretations not to be perfect?

Conclusion

Questions remain regarding how to help such patients. Can one listen and observe in the moment to moment interactions something shifting, that is, the appearance of depressive anxieties, both in the patient and the analyst – that can gradually acquire more expression? Does one observe the construction and shifting in psychic structure that supports a change in the internal world? Does this come about via the interpretation of the shifts that go back and forth in the interaction that takes place in the consulting room?

The experience of being in close proximity to the analyst, and his mind may paradoxically, lead to the possibility of there being no room for the disturbed and damaged aspects of Ms. A, since in her mind they are experienced as intolerable to bear for the analyst. As a consequence, this may create a fear of being expelled or replaced as with a child who mysteriously disappears with no mention, joining the experience of her having been banished as a child from the parents' bedroom. Her resentment for this exclusion makes her seek a perverse vengeance on the analyst and everything that relates to him finding sado-masochistic pleasure in the revenge which substitutes for real analytic intercourse. Yet, at moments where some kind of contact was possible, there was a small and almost unbearable to tolerate shift from this sado-masochistic way of relation to grievance to grief – sadness at what Ms. A can't have.

This patient still found change often largely intolerable, but as the envy, revenge, deprivation and need could be worked through, it seemed to become more tolerable. While she recognized that the perfect combined object union of the anal masturbatory fantasy was not possible to achieve, she found a way of holding onto something of the analyst's, that is, his thinking anal/phallic mind that she can "possess" and will stay with her.

Two dreams seemed to capture this psychic dilemma. In one, a few years into the analysis, the house she lives in is no longer a castle but a cinder block house. In the second one, six months before the end of the treatment Ms. A is very upset at first because her diamond ring, something her mother bequeathed her, has disappeared. She is extremely agitated, but then finds that it has been replaced by a 1 carat diamond instead of the original 4 carat stone.

Carrots, the vegetable, were one of the objects associated with her mother that she used to masturbate with as a child. The ring, something she worshiped and always feared being stolen, is now replaced with another less dramatic, less spectacular object. The manic magical, brilliant object found inside her through her masturbation appears to have changed. She has something of value but it is no longer, either so false or so much the object of envy, hers or others. She also is no longer inconsolable at the alteration of her possessions. They can be more ordinary[6].

A shift from the grievance against the object to grief creates turmoil and chaos in a very rigidly organized psychic organization in which there is a phantasy that everything is already known. When the analyst attempts to help, he causes a disruption and pain that can easily be experienced as sadistic. Change constitutes the greatest threat to the patient's internal stability – a shift in experience and perceptions away from the grievance, threatens chaos. The capacity to move from the persecutory interactions to one in which the bitter resentment gives way to sadness, concern, true longing and eventually a kind of mourning and grieving about one's past is prevented assiduously. The analyst has the difficult task of distinguishing between what is false, "as if" and genuine psychic change.

At the beginning of analysis, Ms. A had a severely limited ability to tolerate any psychic pain and sadness. She felt this was due to the death of her mother, many years before. She would use that inheritance and have her mother pay for the analysis. As she became increasingly aware of her dismissive attitude toward the analysis and analyst, she allowed for something new to touch her without it being constantly destroyed. The pleasure at times of being an analyst was slowly allowed to emerge. Ms. A was able to tolerate the analyst's 'cruelty' of having his own existence without it being experienced as his feeling superior or excluding her.

For A., the painful experience of psychic change appeared to occur through the slow building of her capacity to tolerate despair, loneliness and differences, which, in turn, allowed her to begin to develop genuine concern for an object who might not adore only her. Her need to triumph over her objects diminished somewhat. There was not the perfect coming together where there is only room for one. But working together for a different goal.

Elie Weisel in a discussion called the Anatomy of Hate (1989) speaks of Nietzsche's proposition: that it is not doubt but certainty that leads to madness. It is this struggle that keeps our patients who suffer so greatly from grievances stuck in the analysis, in their past that has become their everyday existence.

Notes

1 Although I have seen a number of patients who share their tendency to express their grievances, this paper will focus on Ms. A. My experience with two others, Ms. D and Ms. M, have been incorporated to some degree within the theory described in this chapter. Yet the clinical work is only from Ms. A's analysis. The similarities have shown themselves to be remarkable, in terms of the overwhelming struggle with analytic change and allowing new 'information' to help bring about this change.
2 This is a reference to the door opening in much the same way that C.S. Lewis describes entry into the world of Narnia in *The Magician's Nephew*.

3 I would refer you to the Irish film 'Butcher-Boy" for one graphic example amongst many based on the novel by. Patrick McCabe's 1992.

4 The word 'grieve' was used in the distant past as a noun meaning an overseer who would cause and inflict pain on others, such as children or slaves.

5 This was the first case in which I had heard what Meltzer (1966) had described in his early paper on Anal masturbation.

6 This is from an observation Betty Joseph made about this case in the middle part of the analysis. It also is reminiscent of Freud's idea paraphrased as turning neurotic misery becoming common unhappiness.

References

Applegarth, A, personal communication.

Berlin, Isaiah, (2000). *The Proper Study of Mankind*. Farrar, Straus and Giroux, New York.

Britton, R., Feldman, M., O'Shaugnessy, E., Segal, H. & Steiner, J. (1989). *The Oedipus Complex Today: Clinical Implications* 54:1–150. Karnac Books, London.

Britton, Ronald. (1989): "The missing Link: parental sexuality in the Oedipus complex " in *The Oedipus Complex Today:Clinical Implications*. 103–128 Karnac Books. London.

Caper, R. (1997). A Mind of One's Own. *International Journal of Psychoanalysis* 78:265–278.

Feldman, Michael. (1989) "The Oedipus complex:manifestations in the inner world and the therapeutic situation", in *The Oedipus Complex Today:Clinical Implications*. 103–128 Karnac Books. London.

Feldman, M. (2008). Grievance: The Underlying Oedipal Configuration. *International Journal of Psychoanalysis* 89:743–758.

Joseph, B. (1985). Transference: The Total Situation. *International Journal of Psychoanalysis* 66:447–454.

Joseph, B. (1992). Psychic Change: Some Perspectives. *International Journal of Psychoanalysis* 73:237–243.

Joseph, B. (1989). *Psychic Equilibrium and Psychic Change: Selected Papers of Betty Joseph*. Psychic Equilibrium and Psychic Change: Selected Papers of Betty Joseph edited by Feldman, M. & Spillius, E. B. 9:1–222., Routledge, London.

Joseph, B. (1986). Envy in Everyday Life. *Psychoanalytic Psychotherapy* 2:13–22.

LaFarge, L. (2006). The Wish for Revenge. *The Psychoanalytic Quarterly* 75: 447–475.

Lansky, M. R. (1994). Shame: Contemporary Psychoanalytic Perspectives. *Journal of the American Academy of Psychoanalysis* 22:433–441.

Lewis, C. S. (1955). *The Chronicles of Narnia: The Magician's Nephew*. Macmillan, United Kingdom.

Meltzer, D. (1966). The Relation of Anal Masturbation to Projective Identification. *International Journal of Psychoanalysis* 47:335–342.

Segal, H. (1994). Phantasy and Reality. *International Journal of Psychoanalysis* 75:395–401.

Segal, H. (2006). Reflections on Truth, Tradition, and the Psychoanalytic Tradition of Truth. *American Imago* 63:283–292.

Steiner, J. (1996). Revenge and Resentment in the 'Oedipus Situation'. *International Journal of Psychoanalysis* 77:433–443.

Steiner, J. (2018). Time and the Garden of Eden Illusion. *International Journal of Psychoanalysis* 99:1274–1287.

Strachey, J. (1934). The Nature of the Therapeutic Action of Psycho-Analysis. *International Journal of Psychoanalysis* 15:127–159.

Spillius, E. B. (1993). Varieties of Envious Experience. *International Journal of Psychoanalysis* 74:1199–1212.

Weisel, Elie. (1989). The Anatomy of Hate. *The Open Mind.*

3 The relevance of Meltzer's contributions to contemporary psychoanalytic practice and its ethical dimension

Cláudio Laks Eizirik[1]

The analytic relationship provides the stage for our patients to share with us the story of their lives and their psychic suffering, as well as the history of their intimate bonds, their aggressive bonds and their inevitable solitudes. There have been many contributions to the characterization of the analytic relationship. In my view, Melanie Klein's, Bion's and Meltzer's concepts and insights inaugurated a new paradigm, jointly with Racker's (1953) and Baranger and Baranger's (1961) key notions of countertransference and the analytic field have allowed present-day analysts to work more closely with the emotions in each session and with deeper analytic material (Eizirik, 2013).

As it is widely known, Donald Meltzer's creative contributions to psychoanalysis include, among others, the aesthetic conflict, intrusive identification, pseudo-maturity, adhesive identification, the preformed transference, a reappraisal of Melanie Klein's discovery of the combined internal object, the claustrum, the utmost importance of individual creativity and the view of psychoanalysis as an art.

As time goes by, not only seasoned analysts who had the unique experience of listening to his lectures, supervise with him and work in his clinical ateliers, but also new generations of analysts bear witness of the lasting influence and growing relevance of Donald Meltzer's concepts and of his way of being a psychoanalyst and to practice what he described once as the most interesting of conversations.

In this chapter, I will describe the way in which I consider the presence of many of Donald Meltzer's insights in our current analytic practice. I will illustrate this with some fragments of sessions. Moreover, I will also explore the way in which his lively presence helped to shed light on the ethical dimension of our impossible profession.

In his seminal book *The Psycho-Analytic Process* (1967), Meltzer describes several successive moments of this complex process, which he calls the gathering of the transference, the sorting of geographical confusions, the threshold of the depressive position and the weaning process, successive

DOI: 10.4324/9781003441861-4

moments that we can identify in our current analytic work. Another extremely creative development of Donald Meltzer is the notion of the aesthetic conflict (Meltzerand Williams 1988), which I will consider next.

On contemporary psychoanalytic clinic

In his remarkable book with Meg Harris Williams, *The Apprehension of Beauty* (1988), Meltzer described the continuous working through of the aesthetic conflict, between the perceptible – the exterior of the object – and the conjectural, the internal, the unknowable of the object, this working through promotes creativity which is a highly desirable achievement, as well as understanding child development, that is also seen by him as aesthetically beautiful.

I will highlight some of the ideas put forward in the chapters dealing with the aesthetic conflict, and then I will offer my own thoughts about each of them.

> Our lives are greatly occupied by relationships which are not intimate. Rousseau's Social Contract well describes the way in which we move about the world, using the lubrication of manner and custom, of conformity and social invisibility to minimize the friction and thus the wear and tear on our psyche-soma...The 'hostage of fate' aspect of our posture towards the casual world of teeming humanity, where everything threatens the head that I love, intimidates us beyond our wildest imaginings...We strive to create, through our apparent docility to the requirements of the community, a private space in which to enjoy the usufruct of our inheritance without let or hindrance.
>
> (Meltzer, 1988, p. 15)

> We wish to prepare our children for the beauties of intimacy but our anxieties for their survival overcome our judgement so that we find ourselves joining in the training process, knowing quite well that it will dampen their thirst for knowledge and constrict their openness to the beauties to which they stand to heir.
>
> (Meltzer, 1988, p.16)

In my view, Meltzer offers here a sober and realistic view of one of the most tragic aspects of human life: the search for intimacy, and the many difficulties involved in reaching it, both due to what he describes at the social level that conspires against intimacy, as well as the individual emotional development with all sorts of inner struggles, fears and inhibitions. I understand that Meltzer is highlighting here several aspects of the "way we move about the world", and the social constraints that prevent the emotional freedom which can stimulate us toward achieving intimacy within ourselves and with others. What is implicit here is the unavoidable conflict between the individual and the world we live in, and the role of education and its institutions between stimulating the freedom to think independently and to develop creativity versus the need to submit to rules, prescriptions and constraints. This conflict can also be seen in psychoanalytic training institutes as well as in psychoanalytic societies (Eizirik, 2023).

> The ordinary beautiful devoted mother presents to her ordinary beautiful baby a complex object of overwhelming interest, both sensual and infra-sensual. Her outward beauty, concentrated as it must be in her breast and her face, complicated in each case by her nipples and her eyes, bombards him with an emotional experience of a passionate quality, the result of his being able to see these objects as 'beautiful'....He (the baby) has, after all, come into a strange country where he knows neither the language nor the customary non-verbal cues and communications. The mother is enigmatic to him; she wears the Gioconda smile most of the time, and the music of her voice keeps shifting from major to minor key... Even at the moments of most satisfactory communication, nipple in mouth, she gives an ambiguous message, for although she takes the gnawing away from inside she gives a bursting thing which he must expel himself. Truly she giveth and she taketh away, both of good and bad things. He cannot tell whether she is Beatrice or his Belle Dame Sans Merci.
>
> (Meltzer, 1988, pp. 21–22)

> This is the aesthetic conflict, which can be most precisely stated in terms of the aesthetic impact of the outside of the beautiful mother, available to the senses, and the enigmatic inside which must be construed by creative imagination. Everything in art and literature, every analysis, testifies to its perseverance through life.
>
> (Meltzer, 1988, p. 22)

These are fragments of what Meltzer called **the core of his discourse**, after which he presented several of its implications. This lively description of the baby's relation with the mother and her beauty and her enigmatic and frightening aspects are extremely useful to understand emotional development. We can see similar movements in the analytic process, or at different moments of each session, or what happens in analytic supervision, which was another area widely explored and described by Meltzer. It can also be a way of describing each moment of the human life cycle, with its gains and losses, joys and despairs, and the continuous uncertainty that is always with us, as well as the unpredictable and unexpected moments of happiness. With his usual creativity, as well as his wide intimacy with poetry, Meltzer uses here two powerful characters from Dante and Keats, Beatrice and La Belle Dame Sans Merci to illustrate the sublime and the horror, love and death, two opposite faces of the mother that are present, in fantasy and reality, throughout our lives.

> It is more than analogical to say that analysts have the same type of aesthetic conflict in their love affair with the psychoanalytical method and its framework of theory of the personality and therapeutic process. Clearly the method, with its intimacy, privacy, ethics, attentiveness, forbearance, non-judgmental stance, its continuity, open-endedness, implicit readiness for sacrifice on the analyst's part, commitment to recognize errors, sense of responsibility towards the patient and his family – all of which is embodied in the dedication to scrutinize the transference-countertransference process – all of these facets, bound together by systematic effort, make the method unequivocally an aesthetic object.
>
> (Meltzer, 1988, pp. 22–23)

It is well known that Meltzer expressed many times his criticism of formal institutional analytic training, as he did in this chapter. However, in spite of this criticism, he continues to be one of the most influential analytic thinkers, and his ideas are included in the majority of the curricula of IPA Institutes.

One of the main points made by Meltzer (1988) is that our theories are essentially retrospective. We are, according to him, explaining, and then we begin to believe our language of "because" and forget what hind sights we are expressing, and we fall into militant elitist groups using the same words, becoming vulnerable to our external and internal critics. Furthermore, stresses Meltzer,

> the teaching of psychoanalysis has taken an institutional form which has perpetuated these elitist groupings and created what Bion would call the Fight-Flight Basic Assumption mentality between groups and a Dependency Basic Assumption (meaning that the group is always hoping and waiting for a better, stronger leader to save them from the mess; the group is passive, and leaders are replaced time and time again) within each… Consequently, the shibboleth significance of jargon words has tended to replace their clinical descriptive meaning as derived from the aesthetic quality of the method.
>
> (Meltzer, 1988, p. 24)

This is a criticism based on what Meltzer observed during his long analytic journey, and in my view it can be seen today in many psychoanalytic institutions. However, I consider that in recent decades there have been new developments in psychoanalytic teaching, the acknowledgement of the three training models, the opening of new tools and ways of training, the growing acceptance of a more pluralistic theoretical approach as well as an active participation of analysts in training so that, partly due to Meltzer's criticisms, but perhaps mainly due to the work of new generations, what we have today is a more complex scenario, more open to accept diversity and different ways of becoming and remaining an analyst (Eizirik, 2011a,b).

What seems to me more interesting here is the way Meltzer reflects on the aesthetic conflict in the love affair we all have with the psychoanalytic method and its setting. I would include here the love affair, comprising love and hate, idealization and paranoid anxieties and all sort of ambivalent feelings and fantasies about Freud and our main authors. Meltzer helps us to acknowledge the need to continuously work through all the aspects of this peculiar love affair. It is perhaps even more difficult to remain an analyst than to train to be one, given the countless temptations to be less rigorous in the difficult work of addressing the unconscious within an analytic field that requires constant maintenance and protection.

Once the formal steps of institutional training are complete, each analyst follows his/her own steps in the midst of addressing the vicissitudes of personal and professional life cycle, facing not only the difficulties of demanding clinical work, but the circumstances of a culture that challenges the relevance and validity of psychoanalysis. Remaining an analyst means being able to tolerate attacks and challenges that emerge naturally from patients and from one self through emotional suffering, as well as an often ambivalent external reality. Remaining an analyst means to be able to move between tradition and innovation without denying the inevitable fluctuation of mental states or the losses and gains of each stage of the life cycle. Since analysts potentially work for longer than other professionals, the aging process deserves special attention, not only because of the limitations it can bring, but because analysts, as they age, may gain greater clinical acuity and courage in dealing with close analytic contact and working with more primitive levels of the mind. Analytic institutions can play an important role in this process, they maintain programs that could be referred as continuous, stimulating psychoanalytic training. Despite the inevitable disappointment of many analysts with their institutions, I still observe that a feeling of "us", a certain sense of belonging and pride in the achievements as a community of psychoanalysts, that can be obtained through joint work, are elements that have the potential of having a containing function that diminishes the different types of anxiety faced by analysts (Eizirik, 2018). Moreover, taking into account what I just quoted from Meltzer, the experience of the psychoanalytic method as an aesthetic object remains a powerful source of inspiration and strength to face all these challenges.

The tragic element in the aesthetic experience resides, not in the transience, but in the enigmatic quality of the object...

(Meltzer, 1988, p. 27)

It is necessary for our understanding of our patients, for a sympathetic
view of the hardness, coldness and brutality that repeatedly bursts
through in the transference and countertransference, to recognize
that conflict about the present object is prior in significance to the host
of anxieties over the absent object.

(Meltzer, 1988, p. 29)

There are several dimensions to be considered concerning this important
point: the meaning of trauma and the repetition compulsion versus what is
being experienced in the present in each relationship and in the process of
development; the consideration of past events in the establishment of psychopathology versus the utmost importance of current life experiences; the
consideration of history versus the emotional experience in the here and
now of the transference in the analytic field, as stressed by Bion, Meltzer,
Baranger and Baranger, Ogden and Ferro; the different meanings of the
concept of transference, still considered by some analysts as the reliving of
past events in the analytic relation versus the living emotion that is aroused
and jointly created by patient and analyst in each moment of the session.

In my view, Meltzer is highlighting here one of the most dramatic shifts,
as I mentioned earlier, in the way many analysts consider what is the essence of psychoanalytic work, considering that it is the constant challenge
and invitation to work with the enigmatic quality of the object, the enigmatic quality of the analytic field and its almost endless possibilities.
In his brief and inspiring paper on transience, Freud (1916), in a subtle
way, opened the door for our possibility of thinking beyond what is lost,
without losing hope, believing that beauty, goodness and the strength of
live can prevail. Meltzer developed ways of trying to make it a reality in
analytic work.

I would like to illustrate some of the notions I had summarized and
commented with clinical material from the analysis of a young patient
who is a photographer that had a well-developed artistic sensibility. Her
analyst is a very gifted and talented person, who was able to dive with the
patient in her several different fantasies and dreams. In the analyst's view,
this material illustrates the notion of aesthetic reciprocity (Meltzer, 1988),
where she is searching predominantly to follow Meltzer's suggestions of
describing the patient's mind as opposed to following the more explanatory model developed by Freud and Klein, as I already mentioned.

In the previous session before the one I will present, the patient was en-
thusiastic with her recent achievements, after having experienced a long
period of what she called psychic paralysis. Her enthusiasm involved her
having moved to a new apartment, a regained impetus in her work, and

a new love relationship. Analyst and patient had resumed in person sessions, after the long pandemic period.

Session:

P: Yesterday I slept at my parents home to take care of their dog, they are away. I can't organize myself there. Yesterday I was waiting for the response from that guy on Tinder I started talking to. It pissed me off not to have a response from him, I keep logging into the app hoping to find something, a follow-up to the conversation with him. What if he didn't find me interesting? I put my best photos, my best angles. (Silence.) I made a plan to organize myself at work, I was procrastinating today and didn't follow the plan. I get irritated with that too.

A: Perhaps you are very afraid that the change and evolution of recent times will weaken, not be sustained.

P: That relationship page, which I decided to reopen after a while, made me rediscover who I was. I am unresponsive and distressed. How come he didn't like me? Is he with someone else? Men don't get involved with me, but they get involved with other women. It irritates me that the creature doesn't enter the chat with the same energy as I do. On the one hand, I'm proud of what I'm achieving, profession, apartment, seeing friends again, but on the other hand it's frustrating not having this valued on Tinder, this not being there visible to anyone who looks at my profile. I know the person has only seen half a dozen photos, but still, I feel disapproved. (Silence.) I dreamed that I was with my mother on a road. She would stop the car because there was a policeman who needed help. And it was a robbery, a trap. My mother handed over the key, they asked, and I thought my computer was in the car, but there was nothing I could do. The important thing was that we got out alive. It was the second time in the month that my mother's car was stolen, something that was repeated. (Silence.) I heard your heavy breathing now and I thought you were trying hard, concentrating. I connected with what it must be like for you to focus all day, work hard, now that I am also working and doing things in my days. How does your head feel after a whole session, after having to go into another session? (Silence).

A: It seems that you're asking yourself if I'm a policeman or a criminal, if it's a trap, if I'm available.

P: I dreamed about you, I don't remember well. They were strange things, not nice, so I forgot, I guess. Something sexual, or you saying things that let me down. But I don't remember anything, just the discomfort. (Silence.) How did I feel so moved by a story as banal as this Tinder one? (Long silence).

A: Where did your mind go?

P: I kept thinking about this feeling of melancholy, of getting excited about the possibilities, the new world, seeing myself with different eyes. And then I find myself more selective with guys on Tinder. I like to be selective, I don't want "any little thing" anymore. But there is a concern.

A: You mentioned post-improvement melancholy. Everything is working out and you ask yourself: "What am I going to do with this childish side of me, which feels inadequate, rotten?". You put the feeling of inadequacy into the Tinder situation. But I invite you to bring back that part that you put there, let's talk about your feeling of worthlessness.

P: Yeah... I had already seen this guy and talked to him on a birthday many years ago, and I didn't want to hang out with him. Now I found it on Tinder and we started talking, until he stopped the conversation and disappeared. This situation of not wanting it back then and wanting it now, having reassessed my criteria, makes it even more difficult to be ignored. For him to get on my interest, I had to re-evaluate.

A: He entered at playoff (laughter)

P: Yes! (Laughter) And even the playoff guy didn't like me. He even replied to my message, but still didn't follow up on the chat. I already read how he wasn't valuing me enough, available.

A: Maybe you're also afraid that I'm not a very secure figure: you think I'm having to make an effort to concentrate on you, in the dream I do things that disappoint you, scare you.

P: I put you in that guaranteed place in my mind: someone who listens to me, is attentive. Then I ask myself: am I not too calm in this relationship with her? Will she let me down? Do I not relax too much here, do I need to be more careful? Last year I spoke with D (colleague) about my work and she gave opinions that left me insecure, I didn't like it. This contaminated our relationship, I became disenchanted, I fell out of love with her. This dynamic happens over and over again in my friendships, this disappointment. As much as I am more closed, I always think that I am the person who loves more, who gives more, who plays more, and others let me down.

A: And you feel that with me also?

P: It is expected so. You have many patients, but I only have one analyst. I wanted to be the only one, the most special one. But you hear many stories besides mine. I don't feel a one-off frustration with you.

A: (A film of the analysis plays in my mind, I remember the intense symptoms she had at the beginning. I think of her interest in my mental processes at work and how much more easily she is accepting when I return her projective aspects. The improvement brings melancholy, envy, insecurity, fear of dependency – I decide to intervene in the pair.). I was here thinking... How many movements have been set in motion here since we started to relate to each other! Our duo experienced so many feelings, experiences, thoughts, to the point of culminating in this psychic post-pandemic phase, spring, in which we are. It's hard to think and tolerate that we depend on each other to work together. Maybe our joint creative ability is making you feel also envious.

P: Yes! It's hard to have pairs like that outside of analysis, in real life. I've never had this intimacy that I have with you with anyone, the encounters I've experienced have never been as transformative as ours. I felt more diminished in relationships, now I see myself growing, increasing potency. I want to believe that this can exist, but I've had more than ten serious boyfriends and I've never experienced that with anyone, just in analysis with you.

A: This is the melancholy…

Q: In a series that I watch, the guy says that nobody has healthy relationships, that this is something they try to sell us. I believe that all relationships have toxic parts, but I believe that it is possible to have a relationship in which the healthy parts predominate, which makes us feel full, powerful, more than anguished. Relationship attempts destabilize me. I go on a road excited, happy, and then this ingredient of relationships, love and sex life comes in, and I feel like a runaway car. These dream robbers are men in general. I decide to stop the car because I think it's worth approaching. But it turns the game, it becomes dangerous, they take something that is mine.

A: Let's not forget that it was your mother who came down.

P: I've been dreaming a lot about my mother, she's always with me.

A: I think because you feel safer with her. But you know that in order to grow you need to question her judgment, the security she gives you. To judge and decide with your own eyes.

P: Yes, I have been disappointed with my mother's suggestions for my problems, the answers she gives to the things I ask. It's not the answers themselves, but realizing that we're different, that we don't think alike. So many times we talk about it here between the two of us, right? I used to feel so alone when you didn't give me the answers. Now I appreciate it, because I think I am finally exercising that muscle and I can see it my own way, not with my mother's eyes, who sometimes lead me to ambushes. And also not with your eyes.

The underlying unconscious fantasy seemed to be that growing up would be boring, losing creativity. In this session, we see a patient who still needs analysis, and perhaps will need it for a long time, but who can now afford to dispense with the blind belief in the mother/analyst's guidelines and already dares to take steps on her own toward independence. The analytic relationship can be an important transformative and intimate experience, as we can see in the fluid dialogue between patient and analyst, and in the latter's reveries.

When we discussed this session, as well as the following one, both the analyst and I felt that this was a period with some characteristics of what

Meltzer (1967) described as the threshold of the depressive position: the material of the sessions reveals the activity of the destructive infantile part fighting a last-ditch stand to preserve the remnants of narcissism by cynical attacks on the truth, with depressive anxieties with distrust, mockery and jealousy-provoking innuendo; complaints around central themes like parents abandoning their children to indulge sexually and analysts abandoning their patients at week-ends and holiday; out-of-sight is out-of-mind; parents and analysts only look after their children because they must by law, custom, reputation and money; if parents and analysts loved their children and patients they would be more concerned to keep them happy. The central problem of this phase of analysis is the establishment of trust in the capability of the good objects, to perform their function of reparation and protection, while still withstanding attacks from bad objects and destructive parts of the self. According to Meltzer there is a repeated rhythmic experience of destruction and restoration, of despair and hope, of mental pain and joy, which makes possible that the experience of gratitude arise, from which the bond of love for, and concern about, the good objects forge. In Meltzer's words

> as the depressive position is penetrated more deeply, the threshold problem of being able to accept forgiveness by good objects for attacks and defections becomes replaced by the problem of being able to forgive oneself for past breaches of good faith.
>
> (1967, p. 41)

The ethical dimension of psychoanalysis

The ethical dimension encompasses the field of our relations with others, mediated, explicitly or implicitly, by ethical codes, for the legitimization of behavioral patterns. However, this ethical dimension involves human beings in continuous relations, relations to us and to others. The metaphorical image of the ethical dimension is the home, the place where we live. Etymologically, ethos is the root of habit, practice and home. Home is a place of shelter, hosting the conditions for the possibility of protection, food and pleasure. To take ownership of our work is to gain some kind of serenity to experience life outside the shelter, to experience challenges and possibilities of the double condition of existence, being thrown into a world that is not chosen, and to recognize the need to build an inside and an outside world that we can be in. Relations with others are built in this middle space, where there is reliability and risk, differentiation and protection, responsibility and challenges (Figueiredo, 1995).

I will take advantage of this metaphor of the home, the place where we live, to expand it into a wider psychoanalytic sense: we live in an external and in an internal world; in our mind and in our body, in the past and in the present; in our dreams, when we are asleep or awake; in the love relations we had throughout life, the ones we have today, the ones we wish we will still have or that we regret we never had; we live in the lives, fantasies, dreams and memories that our patients share with us; in the psychoanalytic method; in our institutions; in the cities we once lived, or we live today, or the ones our parents and forebears once lived, or that we only imagine and so on.

Among many contributions to the study of ethics, Foucault highlighted that it is not possible to take care of yourself without knowing yourself; self-care is self-knowledge – seeking foundations in Socrates and Plato – but also knowledge of rules of conduct or principles that are, at the same time, truths and prescriptions. Taking care of yourself is appropriating these truths. The person who has a beautiful ethos (which is reflected in his habits, his bearing, the way he walks, the calm with which he responds to events), this person, who is the one that is cited as an example, is someone who practices freedom, but in order to have this beautiful ethos one needs to work on oneself.

Foucault uses the concept of self-care to research the way in which a subject can constitute himself (Eizirik, M, 2013).

Foucault points out that, for the Greeks, it is not by taking care of others that a person is ethical. Self-care is also ethical in itself, but it implies complex relationships with others. In addition, self-care also implies a relationship with another, since, in order to take care of oneself, it is necessary to listen to the lessons of a leader. You need a guide, a counselor, a friend, someone who will tell you the truth. Care for others should not be put before care for oneself; self-care ethically comes first, as the relationship with oneself is ontological (Eizirik, M, 2013).

Emmanuel Levinas thinking shows an attempt to conceive the being, breaking with the traditional circle of classical philosophy that does not conceive the other as part of a relationship. Levinas's conceptualization of what is ethical does not back away in the face of challenging and conflicting social, political, religious, economic and ethnic realities, realities that are strongly marked by the absence of ethics as responsibility. His humanist stance emphasizes that we are responsible for the other, who is exposed in his nakedness to violence, pain, hunger, death and extermination produced by the exacerbated greed of possession and power.

He develops a conceptualization of an ethics of care in an individualistic society. His radical ethics of responsibility for the other does not demand any reciprocity. It is only through this total and infinite responsibility that the self can strip itself of its dominating imperialism and welcome the other. But this responsibility, which turns the selfishness of the self inside out, does not destroy it. On the contrary, it bears witness to the central place occupied within ethics by the person who is not himself except by putting himself in the place of the other (taking the faults and sufferings of the other as his own), something no one could do in his own place (Lévinas, 1961).

Turning now to psychoanalytic authors, Freud (1915, 1933) points out that, built on the renunciation of instinctual satisfaction, civilization demands the same renunciation from each person, highlighting that our conscience is not the inflexible judge that professors of ethics declare, but it is, in its origin, social anxiety and nothing else. Studying the beginnings of civilization, the origin and nature of moral conscience in man and the price paid in terms of suffering and psychic illness by the interdictions and drive renunciations that make this same civilization possible, Freud affirms that ethics implies a limitation of drive satisfaction. Freud compares this inhibition of drive satisfaction to that of a person living beyond his means, he describes it as hypocrisy; considers, therefore, that civilization is founded on this hypocrisy. The inescapable conclusion is that civilization rests on a very dubious foundation, it is fragile and unstable, as we continually see, indeed, in analytic rooms, in families and social groups and in different nations, as we are witnessing every day.

According to Andre Green (2007), as Freud theorizing evolved, he increasingly emphasized the importance of the death drive and of destructiveness. Consideration and respect for the other, and for the species itself, is something foreign to this aspect of the human being, which is a source of great disappointment. Another element highlighted by Freud, which has to do with ethics, is that the analytical work is founded on love and the recognition of truth.

Bion (1991) took the question of ethics further: in his digestive model of the mind, he considers truth as the food of the apparatus for thinking which, without it, suffers from starvation. Now, this way of conceptualizing truth turns out to be an ethical imperative that applies to our relationship with the patient and with ourselves. But truth, needs to take into consideration necessary conditions to be received and contained by the other, otherwise its imposition could be an act of violence. Thus, the love of truth needs to be associated with consideration for the other, so that its use does not become arbitrary.

According to Meltzer (1992), the main aspects of an ethical attitude compatible with psychoanalytic principles consists in following, not leading, the search for the (unattainable) truth; building and preserving a framework in which this can occur; enabling the patient's evolution without imposing goals; seeking the meaning and not the exercise of moral judgment on conduct; be prepared for the personal sacrifice of pursuing these aspirations, without imposing these sacrifices on others; restrict the influence of oneself on the patient to the clarity that the communication radiates and not to the action; speak truthfully.

Ogden (2005) highlighted some values that he would not part with, referring to those ways of being and ways of seeing that characterize the distinctive manner in which each of us practices psychoanalysis. He considers these values fundamental for the practice of psychoanalysis, favoring the search of truth and authenticity in the patient. These values are:

being humane; facing the truth; being accountable; dreaming oneself into being; thinking out loud and not knowing.

A personal look at psychoanalytic ethics

Taking into account what I described and discussed previously mainly about some of Meltzer's contribution, as well as other authors, and after thousands of hours flying through the most diverse scenarios of the drama of human existence, I think it is possible to have a more realistic, less idealized or pessimistic view of the undeniable, and sometimes unpredictable possibilities as well as inevitable limitations of psychoanalysis. Below is my current view of psychoanalytic practice and ethics today.

Psychoanalysis is both a science and an art

There are elements of science in psychoanalysis, such as its theoretical foundations, its theory of technique, the analytical method itself with its invariants, its ability to be replicated and produce therapeutic effects or transformations or psychic change. And there are elements of psychoanalysis as an art, which make each analytical relationship something unique and unrepeatable, each analytical session always something potentially surprising and unpredictable, each moment of the session something that is built by two minds that seek to be alive and creative. This unpredictable nature, being both with its necessary simplicity and stability, led Meltzer (1967) to highlight the mysterious function of creativity that can arise in the analytical relationship, and mainly, through his ideas about the aesthetic conflict and the apprehension of beauty to provide evidence of the artistic nature of our method. It is worth noticing that Ogden named one of his books This Art of Psychoanalysis. Thus, an ethical attitude seems to me to imply the acceptance of the inevitable oscillation between these two fields, without having to deny the complexity of this two-fold condition.

Psychoanalysis is a treatment

One can never emphasize enough that when we refer to psychoanalysis, we are talking about a treatment, and as such it is necessary to consider indications, motivation, counter-indications, psychopathology, and the emotional availability and clinical experience of each analyst to accept and start the analysis of each patient. As far as analysts in training are concerned, I think that their personal analysis is the central element of analytic training. This analysis requires a lot of experience from the analyst, a deep analytic identity and identification with psychoanalysis, and a "disposition to maternity", as described by Chasseguet-Smirgel (1988): the ability to wait and see a relationship develop, in a slow, patient daily work, which evokes the image of gestation, the creation and development of an analytic field, the listening to the various expressions of the unconscious and the vicissitudes of training, and considering that someday a new analyst will be born. And, what is required from the analyst in training? patience, hope, courage to delve into his/her own unconscious, tolerance for not knowing and the ability to listen, feel and think about unknown aspects of him/herself that elicit shame, guilt, hatred and all the loving emotions and destructive drives that inhabit all of us.

The analyst's responsibility is to care for and encourage the individuality, subjectivity, desire and choices of each patient

Everyone who seeks analysis is in a state of great helplessness and emotional fragility, in which idealization and the search for magical solutions tend to dominate the analytic relationship. Both in this initial period and in the later ones, the analyst's function is that of a transitional object in the patient's life, helping him, as the Greeks would say, according to Foucault, or Freud himself, as a kind of accompanying guide in the ascent of a mountain. Or like Virgil, who accompanied Dante, in the Divine Comedy, in his journeys through hell, purgatory and some possible paradises.

The analyst's responsibility is to take care of his own mind and his own body, and to remain aware of his inevitable narcissism and his desire to interfere and shape the lives of his patients, having a continuous eye on his possible neutrality.

Meltzer (1967) describes the practice of psychoanalysis as an act of virtuosity, a combination of artistic and athletic activity. He stressed the importance of the analyst's condition, something different from his skill, his knowledge, his character. In his view, just as an athlete's condition has a background in training and a violinist's background in practice, our condition must have a background in a daily, weekly, term-wise and yearly scheme of activities which are calculated to be in direct and immediate support of our analytic performance. Meltzer considers that there must be a guiding principle, that he suggests should be "strain", balanced but close to the limit. Two other important points, for him, are that the aim is stability and the secret simplicity.

Analytic neutrality is explicitly present both in our codes of ethics and in different theories about the analyst's ethical posture. This is a controversial concept, but I believe it is a central element of the analytic stance. For me (Eizirik, 1993, 2021), analytical neutrality is the position, both behavioral and emotional, from which the analyst, in his relationship with the patient, observes, without losing the necessary empathy, keeping a certain distance possible in relation: (1) to the patient's material and its transfer; (2) countertransference and his/her own personality; (3) One's own values; (4) the expectations and pressures of the external environment and

(5) the psychoanalytic theory(s). Such a position does not imply absence of spontaneity or naturalness, but the recognition that maintaining a certain possible distance in relation to these five aspects is the element that allows us to have an increasing and deeper contact and communication with the patient's internal world, with the objective of achieving the therapeutic purposes that we both propose. A certain possible distance is a purposely ambiguous expression. Admits the need for distance, but recognizes that it is relative; at the same time, as much as possible, it is intended to emphasize that we are dealing with a position that is constantly threatened by internal and external influences, and that we try to keep within the possibilities (Eizirik, 1993).

Today, it is also important to consider the analyst as a person and a citizen, and to discuss a problem that has affected the psychoanalytic movement throughout its history, which is the confusion between the possible neutrality within the setting and our life in the polis, as if the former prevented the later.

After all, we cannot stay or be neutral in the face of psychic suffering, the diverse and almost infinite expressions of the death drive and destructiveness, nor the varied and exciting manifestations of beauty, creativity and the often unbelievable human spirit that resists, courageously, to external and internal attacks, and reappears willing to continue this endless task of living and seeking pleasure and conviviality.

The training of new analysts, with the necessary rigor and care, is an ethical responsibility of the institutions and their members

Analytic training is an area that poses countless ethical challenges to our institutions and to the colleagues involved in this task, which includes the so-called impossible professions named by Freud: educating, governing and analyzing. Solid training requires clear and objective procedures, which should be known by everybody, selection criteria and continuous evaluation of professors and students, consistent and flexible curricula that includes new developments, encouraging participation of analysts in training, inclusion of new authors and ideas produced both in psychoanalytic literature and in scientific and humanistic areas. It is also necessary to discuss, revise and modify selection criteria, in an inclusive and welcoming attitude toward differences and the ability to listen to others.

The utmost importance of a solid analytic training, as well as its many challenges throughout time were discussed by Meltzer (1967), when he wrote that the reason why psychoanalytic activity can be placed on a footing with those of the virtuoso and the athlete is because they all rely absolutely, in the heat of their performance, upon the unconscious, rallied and observed by the organ of consciousness. The constant, daily, challenge to work like this, not only requires the formal training, but the never-ending work of remaining an analyst. And how long, asks Meltzer (1967) can a person endure in this strenuous work without the support of social accomplishment and scientific achievement? Not long, he and we all, can answer.

Final considerations

If the notion of ethos includes the meanings of being, doing, residing, customs, practices and if the various visions of ethics that I have high-lighted emphasize self-care and responsibility for others, we can follow two paths: that of prescription, which leads to codes of procedure, as nec-essary as they are potentially superegoic, and the quest to understand what psychoanalytic ethics would be, after all, and where it is found in the foundations of the IPA (Eizirik, 2011a,b). In this second sense, which is what I have privileged here, I think that the notion of concern and care for oneself and for others is as central as that of responsibility.

We observe the conflict between narcissism and object relations, or be-tween the imperialism of the dominating self and the embracement of the other, as Lévinas would say. These aspects clearly emerge, for example, in the history of psychoanalysis, when we see Freud and his colleagues seeking to reach an agreement to create the IPA, and the facts, conflicts and solutions found to establish, develop and maintain each new psycho-analytic institution through all regions of the world. A common element between these first moments and the successive stages is precisely this dialectical relationship between attempts at organization and rupture, concern with the association and its dismemberment, the search for com-mon elements and the denial of any possibility of coexistence with the other, the different., the foreigner, between attempts to connect and dis-connect, as Green would say (Eizirik, 2023).

If there is anything we can learn though the history of the last cen-tury, which is really just a fragment of the great history of revolutionary ideas that shape the human mind and give it meaning, I think that the ethical foundations of the IPA and of all the societies affiliated to it are embedded in the hard daily work that makes us face disappointments, regressions, conflicts, limitations, resistance which allows one to obtain undeniable gains and psychic changes in the endless process of care and acceptance of responsibility shared with the other. This other is not just the patient in analysis, but the psychoanalytic object itself with its the-oretical, clinical, institutional dimension that also takes into considera-tion culture.

The way we take care of and take responsibility for this elusive, enigmatic, stimulating, often frustrating, always demanding object, which sometimes also shows us its splendor and its ability to produce beauty and reduce psychic suffering, in each analytic field and in each institutional experience, is perhaps the best way to honor the legacy of our great thinkers, like Donald Meltzer.

Note

1 I am deeply grateful to Dr. Marina Bento Gastaud for allowing me to include clinical material of one of her analytic cases in this chapter.

References

Baranger,W, & Baranger, M. (1961-2) La situación analítica como campo dinâmico. Revista Uruguaya de Psicoanálisis, IV(1): 3–54

Bion, W (1991) *O aprender com a experiência*. Rio de Janeiro: Imago. (originally published in 1962).

Chasseguet-Smirgel, J (1988) *As Duas Árvores do Jardim*, Porto Alegre: Artes Médicas.

Eizirik, CL (2018) Contemporary Developments and Challenges of Analytic Practice and Training. In Tylim, I and Harris A. *Reconsidering the Moveable Frame in Psychoanalysis*, London and New York: Routledge.

Eizirik, CL (1993) Entre a escuta e a interpretação: um estudo evolutivo sobre a neutralidade psicanalítica. Revista de Psicanálise-SPPA-Vol. I—n.1: 19–42.

Eizirik, CL (2011a) The IPA administration from 2005 to 2009. In Loewenberg, P & Thompson, N. *100 Years of the IPA*. London: International Psychoanalytical Association.

Eizirik, CL (2011b) L'éthique aux fondements de l'API. In Chervet, B. et Porte, JM. *L'éthique du psychanalyste*. Paris: Presses Universitaires de France.

Eizirik, CL (2013) Intimacy, life cycle and analytic relationship. psychoanalysis. today http://www.psychoanalysis.today (PDF.

Eizirik, CL (2021) Dear candidate. In Busch, F. *Dear Candidate: Analysts from around the World Offer Personal Reflections on Psychoanalytic Training, Education, and the Profession*, London and New York: Routledge.

Eizirik, CL (2023) Developing, holding and containing new psychoanalytic groups. In Junkers, G. *Living and Containing Psychoanalysis in Institutions*. London and New York: Routledge.

Eizirik, MF (2013) O cuidado de si: uma perspective filosófica. In Eizirik, CL & Bassols, AM. *O Ciclo da Vida Humana*, Porto Alegre: Artmed.

Figueiredo, LC (1995) Foucault e Heidegger. A ética e as formas históricas do habitar (e do não habitar). Tempo soc. (online). Vol 7, n.1–2: 136–149.

Freud, S (1974a) Reflexões sobre os tempos de guerra e morte. In Edição Standard Brasileira das Obras Psicológicas Completas de S. Freud, vol XIV, Rio de Janeiro: Imago Editora (originally published in 1915).

Freud, S (1974b) Sobre a Transitoriedade In Edição Standard Brasileira das Obras Psicológicas Completas de S Freud, vol XIV, Rio de Janeiro, Imago Editora (originally published in 1916).

Freud, S (1976) Por que a Guerra? Idem, vol. XVIII (originally Published in 1933).

Green, A (2007) Pourquoi les pulsions de destruction ou de mort? Paris, Editions du Panamá.

Lévinas, E (1961) *Totalité et infini. Essais sur l'extériorité*. La Haye: Martinus Nijhoff.

Meltzer, D (1967) *The Psycho-Analytical Process*. London: William Heinemann Medical Books Limited.

Meltzer, D (1992) *Claustrum-una investigación sobre los fenômenos claustrofóbicos*. Buenos Aires: Spatia Editorial.

Meltzer, D and Williams, MH (1988) *The Apprehension of Beauty*. London: The Clunie Press.

Ogden, T (2005) *This Art of Psychoanalysis*. London and New York: Routledge.

Racker, H (1953) A contribution to the problem of counter-transference, Int. J. Psycho-Anal. 34: 312–24.

4 The concept of "claustrum"

A topography of projective identification and negativity in psychoanalytic practice nowadays

Florence Guignard

Introduction

In *"Elements of Psychoanalysis"*, W. R. Bion considers projective identification as being the first element of psychoanalysis; he defines it as "… a dynamic relationship between container and contained".[1]

In his seminal work about the *claustrum*,[2] Donald Meltzer develops the characteristics of container-and-contained in relation to the geography of unconscious fantasy. He investigates the role of pathological projection according to the topography of the container, and the characteristics of the parts of the Self that found a shelter in it.

I shall examine how Meltzer's discoveries might help psychoanalysts to understand today's pathologies and help manage them in their clinical practice. I shall also propose some thoughts about how the concept of claustrum could help us understanding the role of splitting-and-denial, intrusiveness, negativity, lies and violence in nowadays social changes.

Donald Meltzer

Donald Meltzer was undoubtedly an exceptionally gifted psychoanalyst. Privately, Herbert Rosenfeld told me he was "a golden boy", and Otto Kernberg was, jokingly, saying that Don must live in the maternal uterus, as he was able to describe so exactly and pertinently the emotional atmosphere of the primal scene! If we consider Ferenczi as *the wise baby* of our psychoanalytic community, Don Meltzer might well be our *wise fetus,* which is particularly interesting nowadays, as neuroscience discovered that there exists a sensorial memory – named procedural, or implicit – in fetal life, much before birth. As for Bion, he intended to join Don Meltzer and his wife Martha Harris when he returned to England in 1979 after his long stay in California, with the aim of opening a Centre of psychoanalytical research in Oxford. This project sank because of Bion's brutal and unexpected death.

DOI: 10.4324/9781003441861-5

His book *The Kleinian Development*[3] shows his ability to integrate and describe the way of thinking of three geniuses of psychoanalysis: Sigmund Freud, Melanie Klein, and Wilfred R. Bion.

The Claustrum

The Claustrum is the last of Don Meltzer's books published when he was still alive. It is of great interest for several reasons.

In his previous books, Meltzer examined the object relations and identifications in the time-and-space dimensions of the psychic apparatus, talking about the unconscious representations of the "geography of fantasy". In *The Claustrum*, he considers the way in which a subject may use that geographic representation in order to possess at any price the inner spaces of her or his internal maternal object. The subject does this through doting of the qualities, shapes, and ways of functioning create through projective-intrusive identification to the internal maternal object.

Projective identification and negativity

Exploring the phantasmatic territories into which the patient projects parts of his Self, Meltzer develops his views about the interlocking effect of *projective identification*. Whereas, in his previous works, he had mostly written on the *identificatory* aspects of it, Don Meltzer largely develops here the *projective* dimension of such a dynamic concept – a "concept of the third type",[4] dealing with "the-links-between-the-links".

W. R. Bion largely opened the field of this concept by considering its normal functioning as the starting point of the capacity to think. For this author it is normally used between the infant and her mother as the first means of human communication. It is of a particular interest to see Meltzer continuing W. R. Bion's work and investigating closely the pathological aspects of projective identification. He does so after clearly reminding the reader of the difference existing between *pathology* and *immaturity* – namely in childhood and adolescence.

From the viewpoint of *psychopathology*, Meltzer proposes an outstanding description of *negativity* at work in the psychic life of the subject, as well in the drives functioning, as in the projective and identificatory aspects of object relations, and in the various expressions of human character. He also develops in a very new and interesting way the links existing between projective identification and group mentality as a defense against melancholia in perverse patients.

From the viewpoint of the *nature of projective identification*, Meltzer points out here the most intrusive and frightening aspects of it when distorted objects, damaged by the violence of the projective intrusion into them, are reintrojected into the Self. This is already well known through Freud's case of the *Wolf man* and Klein's first description of projective identification. But, in *The Claustrum*, Meltzer goes further, by exploring the concept of *psychic space*, and describing the different spaces of psychic life.

Geography of internal psychic spaces

Don Meltzer's extreme sensitivity enabled him to detect in quite a precise manner and in each clinical situation, the characteristics of the internal object-container in which a patient is contained in fantasy and to evaluate the psychic price the patient pays for this. Meltzer will also consider the therapeutic means possible to help the patient get out of this situation without too many dangers of being lost, dismantled or dissolved. He proposes to describe any analytic session from a phenomenological point of view[5] to get an overview of the geography of unconscious fantasy.

He describes six areas with which the subject is likely to have a relation by means of projective identification: the *external world*, the *maternal uterus*, the *inside of external objects*, the *inside of internal objects*, the *internal world*, and the *delusional system*, which he equates to the *nowhere*. The first five of these areas are endowed with psychic reality. The first – the external world – has no meaning as such, but it can be endowed with meanings projected into it by the inside world of the subject. The sixth one – the delusional system – has no meaning either but for another reason: the qualities attributed by it to phenomena are delusional, and the objects dealt with are bizarre objects.

The relationships of the subject with the *external world*, mainly the material part of it, aim essentially to the purpose of adaptation and have little impact on the development and the transformations of the psychic apparatus. However, by means of projective identification, events and objects of that external world may be endowed with attributes and qualities belonging to the *internal world*. This is particularly true from the point of view of the apprehension of beauty, giving then rise to the aesthetic conflict and the pain linked to uncertainty.[6] The main issue to such a pain consists of splitting the Self capacities to experience emotions. But to reach an adaptive aim, splitting the emotions is not enough, as any perception and reflexion relative to the meaning of the external world includes necessarily a sense of values. So, in order to avoid pain and uncertainty, the subject might use the external world as a locus of intrigue, lies, relating to it with a triumphant attitude, and a group mentality, as described by Bion.[7]

According to Bion, certain infantile parts are abandoned at birth and remain in the *maternal uterus*. These "unborn parts" can contain important capacities to experience emotions and to develop a capacity to think. Besides, the recent discoveries about *implicit memory*[8] confirm Bion's intuition and Meltzer's use of it, namely the important distinction made by Meltzer between these unborn parts, on the one hand, and, on the other hand, the pathological objects projected into the maternal uterus of the internal mother, by means of some violent, even murderous actions of projective identification.

However, just as the phantasmatic relations with the uterine space of the internal mother contain the potential capacity to think, the *negative parts* of these, contain the potential for a *"folie-à-deux"* or for multiple personalities, as well as for an experience of demonian possession.

The relations with the *inside of external objects* allow the subject to express emotions, whereas projective identification to the *internal objects* impacts most levels of the "internal world" and may give the subject its most vivid experiences of the union of truth with beauty.

The world of delusion and of *nowhere* is made of bits and pieces of objects and drives in their worst conditions, both destructive *and* destroyed; needless to say, this is of no use for the psychic development and functioning.

The claustrum

Meltzer's investigations go even deeper. He studies the *intrusive* nature that may endow the subject's projective identification into its *most important internal object*: the *mother's body*. Exploring the places of the maternal space that might possibly be invaded by such an intrusive movement, he considers three of them: *the head/breast, the genitals, and the rectum*. Because of the violence of the intrusion, each of these may become a *claustrum* in which some infantile parts of the Self could remain imprisoned, expressing the characteristics of that place of the mother-body through mimicry, distortion, and denigration.

The first two, the *head/breast* and *the genitals,* give rise to descriptions of interesting pathologies. For the first one it will be expressed through omniscience and grandiosity. For the second one, it will be expressed through sexual excitement and violence, rape, child abuse, and feminicide. Such pathologies might be transient or could also lead the subject to shift from one claustrum to another, from erotism to sadomasochism, which could end in the third one, the most dreadful and hopeless: the mother's rectum. Here we find the kingdom of Orwell's novel "1984", with its pervert injunctions dictated by Big Brother: Evil is Good, Lie is Truth, and so on and so forth… Here we find the realm of group mentality, "both psychopathic and schizophrenic", as Bion qualified it, with its basic assumptions replacing thinking activity, imposing its pervert use of justice, with its law of retaliation, and its seduction maneuvering to take advantage of a friendly invitation for intruding the object.

Meltzer considers such a mode of functioning as the most dramatic aspect of *claustrophobia*. The "capacity to think the thoughts" (Bion) is severely attacked, emotions are reduced to mere excitement, suicidal ideas are permanent, as the subject lost the capacity to represent death. "It is a world of addiction, in which the subject entrusts his/her survival to the good will of a malevolent object" (p.99). The subject becomes a kind of a double agent, cynically hiding its sadomasochistic, filicide perversion under a model of parental care or psychoanalytic method (*sic*)... A beloved object is taken hostage, whose identity is difficult to distinguish, but it is always a child figure.

A place where any psychic development is impossible, such a claustrum constitutes, according to Meltzer, the antechamber of schizophrenia, with only two possibilities to escape it: either expulsion into an unknown space, or entering3 "the no-where of the delusional system" (p.121). Meltzer describes vividly how exhausting it is to survive in a *claustrum*, as an intruder avoiding expulsion in an unknown – hence terrifying – outside, maintaining only manipulative, deceitful, delinquent alliances, never reaching true emotional relations of intimacy without having immediately a negative confabulation nipping in the bud meaning and creativity... this is the destiny of the parts of the Self imprisoned in the claustrum, especially the anal one. Delusional formations might well be seen as a welcome exit.

The primary maternal space and feminine space of development

Such pathologies appear very early in life. In my opinion, they express a deep suffering at the junction between the *primary maternal space* and the *primary feminine space* of development.[9] A model of such a pain could be given by Winnicott's notion related to the infant's experience of mirroring – or not – in the mother's eyes. Suppose that, for any reason, such an experience of identity goes wrong. The consequence will be that the capacity to grow from a fusional start of the capacity to think – in the *primary maternal space* – to the birth of an identity of one's own – in the *primary feminine space* – will not be possible, and the baby will not experience the mother's femininity, which is correlated to separatedness. The baby's projective identification will become more and more intrusive, aiming at recuperating a territory lost forever. The more destructive the subject's intrusion into the mother's territory, the more distorted the container desired. Moreover, the guilt associated to the baby's destructive intrusion will be increasingly persecutory.

As a result of this intrusive destructivity, the internal maternal object is transformed from a soft and osmotic container to a hard, distorted carapace, used as a shield against any experience that might bring the subject to a more individual experience of life, with its emotions, its unexpected events, its questions not always answered, its hopes not always accomplished, and its limited time of existence…

The claustrum in psychoanalytic practice today

How does the psychoanalyst work with a patient whose important part of the Self is imprisoned in a claustrum? Such a situation is always experienced painfully by the analyst in the countertransference, often as an impasse in the treatment. Meltzer focuses his attention on the future of the transference, he points out to a difference between a first analytic experience and a second, third, or even fourth trial of analytic treatment. He observes that it is generally difficult to deal with the transference developed in a previous analysis, generally not solved, but often hidden – consciously or not – by the patient.

These observations appear to be extremely useful in the difficult situation of psychoanalysis in our contemporary world. On the one hand, speed and performance are the gods of today's group mentality, which gives little place to intimacy and curiosity for an internal world. On the other hand, most people take advantage of the remarkable progress in neuroscience, to split and deny the psychic component attached to any neuronal functioning. Nowadays, it is more trendy to undertake all kinds of "short therapies", made of a mixture of physical training and eye-movements, with a behavior guide to "manage" one's emotions as one would do with a bank account, and a final touch of exotic incantations to keep your meditation in well controlled paths, rather than to consult an analyst who encourages the person to remember and tell their dreams and does not explain immediately and once and forever the complete meaning of them, because the analyst needs to listen to the associations to it beforehand; to talk about whatever comes to his or her mind, and then still suggests that you are treating the analyst unconsciously as you used to treat your mother or your father when you were a child…

When psychoanalysis spread in West countries, it brought a welcome dismantling of psychiatric classical nosography, with the idea that a topographic and dynamic point of view on psychic pain would be more accurate and clinically helpful than categories of diagnosis fixed once and forever. But such a way of thinking brought with it too much uncertainty for the so-called "scientific standards" inherited from the nineteenth century. We experience every day that the "negative capability" described by Keats and prescribed by Bion is beyond what is accepted by our present civil societies, this is also true in the field of mental health. This explains why an inventory of so-called "handicaps" is now the only policy accepted by medical administrations. It is easy to code it as a digital information, and its use in communication amongst colleagues avoids the risk of being wrong: there are no diagnosis, hence no hypothesis anymore, prognosis is only given by algorithms based on percentages whose pertinence are often not adequately questioned.

The consequences on the treatment of psychic pain are important, as such a policy imposes to prescribe first one, or more reeducations, made by practitioners who are implicitly advised not to be in any way familiar with psychoanalysis. Then, if any psychotherapeutic help appears fit to help the uncertain or fragile results of reeducations, behavioral therapy is recommended, while any kind of therapy considering the unconscious functioning is preferably discarded.

Thirty years ago, Meltzer expressed his deep concern about the future of psychoanalysis – especially the future of our means to deal with the transference-countertransference lever effect when we are working in a second, third, or even more psychoanalytic situation.

In my opinion, a third component played an important role in Meltzer's discovery of the pathological distortion of the container-contained situation – although he does not mention it explicitly: the psychoanalytic training experience might well play an unexpected role in the resistances of the candidates, a resistance to abandon a certain degree of omnipotence which has as a consequence the development of hard and secret defenses that remain hidden in a maternal claustrum.

Whatever the rules of any Psychoanalytical Society in the world, we know that these will inevitably interfere, for better or for worse, with the personal development of the candidates through their personal analytic treatment. In particular, the model of a container-contained relationship experienced by the candidate with his or her analyst might well be very different from what s/he will find in the relationships between the Training analysts and the candidates of the Society. Scientific, professional, or religious societies are not structured on a family model. This is why group mentality is so easily flourishing in them. Because there is no intermediate territory – like family surroundings for the child, when confronted with the society – the gap will be felt more directly at the primitive levels of object relations-and-identifications.

We might not have measured the strength and determination of the unconscious functioning to regain as many territories as possible over those explored by the psychoanalytic work. We needed several decades of practice and of transmission of psychoanalysis to discover the violence of such a movement of retreat. A decade after Don Meltzer's prophetic book on the *claustrum*, André Green proposed a new concept *"la position phobique centrale"*[10] – the phobic, central position – in which he describes the phobia of psychic life as central to the human functioning.

Today, while considerable modifications occurred in the civil society during the last 40 years or so, we are facing a "catastrophic change", with the recent pandemic which forced lockdown periods, with the increasing number of identity troubles and gender dysphoria, and with war knocking insistently at our western doors. Supremacy of action as a social ideal confronts us with the many phobic issues that lead us to avoid at any price having to look at what happens inside our unconscious psychic life.

After the raise of "borderline" patients, we now observe an important amount of severe pathologies at the level of primary defenses – splitting, denial, idealization, projective identification. These show severe signs of phobic attitude toward psychic life, with violent and perverse defenses, mobilized to stop any psychoanalytical process that would help the subject to get out of its claustral situation. The amount of rage, envy, and paranoid guilt is often too heavy to bear, compared to the genuine capacities to repair possessed by any young child – hence, of by the Infantile of any adult.

Such pathologies do not appear only in borderline or psychotic patients. We also observe them in patients whose neurotic troubles have been dealt with in a first therapy, often an analytic one, or else, in the first part of our analytic work with them.

On the analyst's side: Blind spots and dream activity

When I discovered and described "the blind spots" in the mental functioning of the analytic pair,[11] I did not sort out the *level* of the psychic apparatus on which these blind spots appeared. Now, I see how important it is to do so, as we might have severe "blind spots" in the (claustro)phobic situation as described by Meltzer. We might unconsciously *deny* the negative action on the analytic work, coming from the patient's part hidden in a maternal claustrum. What could appear as a neurotic conflict between the desire to be cured and a normal link to an internal object that must be left – abandoned, mourned – to go on developing, could well be a criminal conspiracy coming from the phobic part of the subject that is determined to stay inside the maternal claustrum and is ready to use any weapon to derail the analytic alliance and to defeat the process of the cure.

To conclude

While I was writing this paper and reading once more Meltzer's vivid description of the difficulties, for the psychoanalyst, to "dig out" the infantile transference of such patients – particularly when they have had already one or more analytic experiences – I had two memories which I propose as a provisional conclusion.

The first one is a nightmare I had during a weekend of work with Meltzer. I communicated it to him during a friendly conversation, and, as the reader will see, I got an unexpected interpretation of it:

The dream: "As I was walking into a hospital where I was working, I witnessed a horrible scene: In an atmosphere evoking the Factory scene of Chaplin's film 'Modern Times', I see doctors and nurses grabbing patients and cutting them into pieces, regardless of their sufferings. They did not pay attention either to my anguished protestations and they pushed me away to continue to butcher".

To my amazement, Don started laughing and said: « That's just the dream of an experienced practitioner of psychoanalysis about what psychoanalysts can do to their patients! »

My second memory is Bion's reaction to the demand of a neurotic patient of mine, who moved from Paris to California after three years of an excellent analytic work; when she asked Bion to continue analysis with him, he had an interview with her and told her at the end of it: *"I don't think you need more analysis. One never spends enough time away from psychoanalysis"*.

Still, it might be necessary to keep on using the *"ignis"* and *"ferraes"* (Freud) of our impossible profession: after all, does not spring keep on coming back, even after the worst of winters?

Notes

1 Bion W. R. 1963 *Elements of Psychoanalysis*, William Heinemann Medical Books LTD, chap. 1, p. 3.
2 Meltzer D. 1992 *The Claustrum. An Investigation of Claustrophobic Phenomena*. With an essay by Meg Harris Williams: "Macbeth's Equivocation, Shakespeare's Ambiguity". Strathtay (Scotland), Clunie Press.
3 Meltzer D. 1978 *The Kleinian Development*: Book I (Freud), Book II (Klein), Book III (Bion). Single-volume edition Perthshire: Clunie Press.
4 Guignard F. 2019 *Psychoanalytic Concepts and Technique in Development. Psychoanalysis, Neuroscience and Physics*. The New Library of Psychoanalysis, London, Routledge Taylor & Francis Group.
5 Merleau-Ponty M. 1945 *Phénoménologie de la perception*. Paris, Gallimard.
6 Meltzer D. & Harris Williams M. 1988 *The Apprehension of Beauty. The Role of Aesthetic Conflict in Development, Art and Violence*, Perthshire, Clunie Press.
7 Bion W. R. 1948 *Experiences in Groups*, London, Tavistock, 1961.
8 Mancia M. 2004 *Feeling the Words. Neuropsychoanalytic understanding of memory and the unconscious*, Engl.translation Judy Baggott, London, Routledge 2007.
9 Guignard F. 2020 *Psychoanalytic Concepts and Technique in Development. Psychoanalysis, Neuroscience and Physics*. London and New York, Routledge. The New Library of Psychoanalysis. Chapter 2: The birth of psychic life, pp. 21–35.
10 Green A. 2000 La position phobique centrale, *Rev. Franç. Psychanal*.t. LXIII, n° 3, 2000, pp. 743–771.
11 Guignard F. 2020 *Psychoanalytic Concepts and Technique in Development. Psychoanalysis, Neuroscience and Physics*, The New Library of Psychoanalysis, London and New York, Routledge. Chapter 13, The-Infantile-in-the-psychoanalyst. Blind spots and stopper-interpretations pp. 200–217.

5   Adolescent symbolic reordering, the expansion of the mind and leaving the claustrum

Ruggero Levy[1]

Summary

Adolescence can be understood as a great symbolization process in which the system of representations of the self and of objects created during childhood fails and has to be reordered/reconstructed during the adolescent process to account for the new body, new impulses and a new perspective of objects and the world. Since the self is a symbolic construction, the failure of the system of representations brings up deep anxieties of annihilation and death. Adolescents use various resources to defend themselves from these primitive anxieties, including intrusive projective identifications in internal objects, characterizing what D. Meltzer described as life in the claustrum.

From a clinical case of a young adolescent girl, I will illustrate the exit from the claustrum through analytical work, as she constructs representations of the prison in which she was imprisoned. As she begins to construct representations of the "leader of the claustrum," this loses its oppressive force and begins to be seen as a representation, losing its tangibility and, therefore, its strength.

Introduction

Adolescence is great period of transformation of the human subject and can be understood from several perspectives. In this article, I examine it from the viewpoint of symbolic processes, understanding it as a great process of symbolization in which the system of representations of the self and of objects created during childhood fails and has to be rearranged/reconstructed during the adolescent process to account for the new body, new drives, and a new perspective of objects and of the world. Since the self is a symbolic construction, the failure of the representation system brings up deep anxieties of annihilation and death. Adolescents use various resources to defend themselves from these primitive anxieties, including intrusive projective identifications into internal objects, characterizing what D. Meltzer described as life in the claustrum.

DOI: 10.4324/9781003441861-6

Symbolic reordering in the adolescent process

The human subject is a being that develops essentially in a symbolic world (Levy, 2001), which is why Cassirer (1997 [1944]) says that humans should not be considered rational animals but symbolic animals. The great dividing line between humans and other animal species, according to Cassirer (1997 [1944]), is the existence of an intermediary symbolic system between the stimulus receptor system and the motor effector. As a symbolic system, thought mediates the immediate reaction, as Freud says in "Two Principles" (1911).

As Cassirer writes, human beings live immersed in the symbolic network created by themselves, literature, the visual arts, religions, science, so that they are no longer able to confront reality directly, face to face,

> Humans live in a symbolic universe. Language, myth, art, religion are parts of this universe. They are the various threads that weave the symbolic net, the tangle of human experience [...] No longer can humans confront reality immediately; they cannot see it, as it were, face to face,

but only through the interposition of that web that they have created themselves (Cassirer, 1997 [1944]).

The adolescent process is no different. It is formed by the disconnection of the previous representation systems assembled by the subject (Cahn, 1999) throughout childhood, and by the creation of a new system of representations that accounts for the new body, the self, objects, and the world. We then witness, through this painful process of deconstruction and reconstruction of a system of representations, the emergence of a new subjectivity in the symbolic universe of the subject, with all the vicissitudes that are typical of such an endeavor.

But why do I not simply refer to the construction of a new identity in adolescence? Precisely because I want to focus attention on what happens metapsychologically in the phantasmatic world of the subject, and accompany this great process of symbolization that is adolescence and a particular type of anxiety that emerges from this process.

The new adolescent body emerging from puberty, with its new forms, new drives, new potentialities, gives the mind an unprecedented amount of work to do. It confronts the adolescent with a disturbing stranger (Cahn, 1999) that needs to be represented internally in order to recreate a sense of familiarity with oneself. As Piera Castoriades-Auglanier (1975) writes, symbolizing means assimilating a "strange body" into a certain system of representations. I refer to "strange body" here in a double sense: as a foreign element that needs to be assimilated, and as a biological body that is foreign to the subject.

What makes this phenomenon even more disturbing is that the troubling stranger troubles not only the subject, but also others, so the surprise of others further reinforces the feeling of strangeness so common in this moment of life. According to Cahn (1999), it is this feeling of strangeness to oneself and to others that gives adolescence the thickness and specificity of its psychic transformations. And to the extent that we are talking about the reordering of the system of representations of self and others, the collapse of one system and the construction of another, in addition to feelings of strangeness we are also confronted with deep anxieties of annihilation, often a sense of imminent death. It is this anxiety I intend to focus on in this paper. The self feels threatened because it is a symbolic construction.

Throughout childhood, subjects construct a system of representations of the self and objects that guarantee them some stability of their self-image. With this radical process of symbolic reordering, besides the loss of childhood and the infant body, there is the loss of the representations of the self and of objects, an experience that causes a feeling of terror. Winnicott (1975 [1951]) said that the greatest psychic suffering exists when one loses not the object, but its representation. At the end of this same work, Winnicott introduces the issue of the negative in psychoanalysis, highlighting that when there is a loss of representation, sometimes the only possible reality of the object is its lack: the only presence of the object is its negative. There are individuals who will cling to lack, absence, and therefore suffering as the only real thing. How is this related to the subject I am addressing? There are adolescents who, faced with the loss of the representation of themselves and faced with the feeling of not existing, will often cling to the negative as the only tangible reality: suffering, pain, being destructive, is a way of being. Others, as I argue at the end of this paper, "appropriate" through an intrusive projective identification (Meltzer, 1992) the identity of a given object and begin to function according to this object.

More recently, Botella (2002) tells us how the traumatic situation occurs because the subject is unable to create representations of a certain experience that can connect the affections that it arouses. In this sense, we can predict that adolescence will be traumatic if the subject cannot recreate a system of representations that account for this new experience and, therefore, fails in this unprecedented experience of subjectivation.

As a result of this symbolic re-ordering, I suggest that mentalization insufficiencies (Marty, 2003 [1990], 1992) are inevitably created in adolescence, to a greater or lesser degree, causing the body to play a central role in the attempt to dominate the anxieties of the period.

A particular mind-body connection is established at this time of life, because, on the one hand, the body demands representation (Aisenstein, 2009) in which the mind should contain the symbolic representations of the new body, the new emotional experiences triggered by it, and the new perception of the world. On the other hand, faced with these insufficiencies of mentalization, the body will often have to "contain" non-symbolized emotions, preventing them from being thrown into the infinity of external reality, returning later in the form of hallucinations typical of psychosis. A particular container/contained relationship is thus established in adolescence. The body presents itself as an intermediate space between the mind and the infinite universe (idem.) of external reality when the mind is still unable to symbolize the infinite new experiences of adolescence.

The attempt to acquire a narcissistic balance

In numerous works (1966, 1973, 1978, 1989, 1992), Meltzer developed the study of mental geography, studying mental spaces, the transit between them, their compartments, characteristics, including their importance in adolescence. He sought to study the various types of projective identification within objects, their communicative, structuring, and defensive purposes.

In *The Claustrum* (1992), Meltzer describes the consequences of these fantasies for the psychism. He differentiates between projective identification, which has more adaptive and communicative purposes, and intrusive identification, with fewer possibilities of reversibility, in which the individual appropriates the object, transforming it, in his fantasy, into a claustrum that imprisons and is no longer a container. These are situations in which the self is dominated in its functioning by this intrusion, determining that the individual's whole sense of identity is compromised. Referring to adolescents, he comments that understanding what intrusion into a claustrum is allows us to observe not only the change in the sense of identity when it occurs, but also to recognize the world that the adolescent is inhabiting.

> the vision of the claustrum illuminates this change in the sense of identity, making it possible to recognize that they are different not only from what they were before, not only in their mental qualities, but also as to the world they are inhabiting.
>
> (Meltzer, 1992, p. 147)

In another work, *Refúgios narcisistas na adolescência* (Levy, 1996), I describe in detail what these mental spaces with structuring and defensive functions are and how they are constituted in adolescence. I describe the destructive aspects involved in these mental organizations and their repercussion on psychoanalytic technique, especially on countertransference.

To defend themselves from their depressive, paranoid, confusion and annihilation anxieties, and especially from this feeling of depersonalization resulting from the symbolic "dismantling" in the adolescent process, young people will psychically transit not only between various communities (the family, the adult world, groups, and isolation; Meltzer, 1978), but also between various objects. Through more or less intrusive projective identifications, parts of the self will "move" through a complex geography, creating more or less transitory identifications with more or less damaging consequences for the self. That is, as adolescents lose the representation of themselves, they seek to "appropriate" some self, some identity.

To intrude inside the object, in fantasy, and inhabit a zone of this object's body, especially in adolescents where zonal and object confusions are particularly important due to the evolutionary process, seems to me to be something central to their psychopathology.

Below I try to illustrate the above, using an excerpt from Iris's analysis, previously used in another work (Levy, 2022).

Iris and the great leader

Our meeting had an impact on me. Iris was tall with dark disheveled hair, dressed all in black, chunky boots, her face partially covered by her hair and, on looking closer, a certain shadow under her eyes. With her blasé manner, she was visibly trying to shock me with her nihilism. She wondered about the meaning of life, the validity of life in society, which reminded me of the idealization of confusion with simulations of creative thoughts. She also idealized a bohemian way of life; she was a bit of a bum, not committed to the "patrician" tasks of the life of a "little bourgeois girls." The fear I felt in my countertransference told me that, besides the histrionic intention of provoking an astonished reaction—which made her feel real and present—there was a real risk of self-destruction. At night, she and her boyfriend had been walking around an area known for prostitution, homeless and destructive drug use.

At the beginning of the session, she talked about her confusion about herself. Deep down she didn't know if she wanted to study, she didn't know if she wanted to go on with her boyfriend or if she was gay, if she wanted to go on with the friends she had had until then, or if she wanted to join a goth group at school, with classmates older than her, who invited her to go out with them... It was clear to me that in the face of this disorientation, the black, the negative, was a relief, because it was something. It was an attempt at relief from the confusion of not knowing what she positively was. At this time, I was trying to grasp and understand the anxiety she was experiencing and to understand how she was defending herself from it. The feelings of unreality she was defending himself from, getting others to react to her appearance or her nonsensical comments. That is, she would appear and say something and when her interlocutor reacted, she confirmed that she was real and that she was there, a fact.

She told me about her adventures with a friend, who was "really crazy." I considered that Carla was a kind of Iris' double in the sense that Iris by projective identification putted into her splitted feelings and parts of herself. The same age as Irene, Carla was the daughter of drug users and an intense drug user herself, not only marijuana but also stimulant pills and alcohol. They also carried out small pranks together at school. We ana-lyzed in Carla, Iris's double, a character in our transitional analytic space, feelings of loneliness, abandonment, and hatred. That is, we examined in this friend—and I understood this was a disassociated aspect of hers—this set of Iris's emotions that were split and projected at that moment.

I thought I should keep calm and, remembering Bion, I should be able to walk before the war tank, enemy fire ahead of me and the tank's treads behind me, containing and transforming the fear. I was watching Iris in her narcissistic refuge, full of omnipotence and destructiveness, which, on the one hand, assured her an identity—a negative one, but an identity nonetheless—but, on the other hand, endangered her health. It was nec-essary to enter this refuge with her, to describe it in detail, to understand it from our experiences in the session, to help her out of this world of sim-ulacra in which she was imprisoned. She lived so trapped in this world she had plunged herself into that she often felt a deep sense of unreality, absent, away from everything and everyone. Sometimes she would ram-ble on about reality and fantasy. Other times she told me in anguish that when people talked to her she felt far away, distant, and that she made fa-cial expressions to give the person the impression that she was following what they were saying. It reminded me of Meltzer describing the world of projective identification. I would try to calm her down and explain to her that this happened because she withdrew into herself, trying to find her-self and distancing herself from others. Other times I managed to show her that she had turned into Carla too much and that she felt she was no longer herself.

But I will go directly to a very creative dream that Iris had recently had, and which she gave me in the form of a text at the end of her analysis.

> I dreamt that I was in a kind of labyrinth, dark, dirty, dripping. It looked like the basement of an abandoned building, full of homeless people, like one I saw in a Batman movie. Like in the movie, music could be heard in the distance and it seemed like a kind of cult, a worship of the head of the underworld. Suddenly I had a sewer pipe pointing at me. I knew that some kind of bullet could be fired from it. I was terrified and could only look at the dark hole. And I knew it was his doing, his gang. That son of a bitch who thinks he's the Almighty of the underground was running everybody's life, corrupting every-body, the politicians, the police, everybody. I was sneaking through the tunnels of the labyrinth, and suddenly I bumped into him. He was trying to kill me. Like in the movie, he was trying to suffocate me. I don't know how, but I managed to escape and run away through the mazes. I kept sneaking around and arrived at a sort of command center, the central place from where he did all his shit. From that un-derground he ruled the city and everyone's lives. I understood that this was the heart of everything, the heart of that shit. And I understood

what needed to be done to end his power and end himself. I molded a doll of that shit out of clay, in almost natural size, smaller than me. I transformed the big boss, who ruled the life of the whole city from the underworld, into an inert clay statue. The incredible thing was that the whole environment fell silent, the prayers stopped. And I left there and went to my house, but I had a clear conscience. But the strange thing was that even though I was done with him, I was calm, I guess with the feeling that I had done what needed to be done.

I believe that this dream speaks for itself. It illustrates the anal and deadly environment in which Iris has been living, her submission to the "big boss," the leader of the rectal claustrum, but mainly her rebellion against this perverse, domineering and cruel object that had taken control of part of herself. Threatened with death, she goes to the heart of the monster, "the command center," and puts an end to him and his power. From the point of view of Oedipal anxieties, one could also say that she needed to "kill" her cruel and domineering childhood father, who instead of seducing her into life, was suffocating her. "*Killing him*" was the way to survive and develop her creative potential.

But perhaps richest of all is the way she ends his power and domination: she turns him into a representation in clay! And notice—a suggestion from my colleague and friend Claudia de Carli—that when clay is wet it is soft, moldable, subject to successive transformations, which perhaps speaks for itself: the old system of representations being recreated in more flexible forms. In other words, as in the analysis she can create representations of this prison that led her precisely to behave according to this boss and to be confused about her identity, she can come out of it and see the "great leader" as a representation in clay. As she is able to represent him, the evil leader seems not only to have lost his strength and power, but can also be seen as something lesser, not so grand and majestic. We see her irony, sarcasm, and a certain manic mood helping her in her confrontation with this cruel and deadly paternal internal object within which she was imprisoned, her dilemmas of conscience, but her absolution in the sense that there was nothing to be done: to survive one had to "kill" the destructive father and identify with his creative objects.

Conclusion

I believe I have demonstrated the vicissitudes of the adolescent process from the point of view of the reordering of the system of representations of the self, of objects, and of the world. This path generates particular anxieties, from which young people try to defend themselves through transitory or more rigid identifications, through more or less intrusive projective identifications.

I believe that Meltzer's references are particularly rich to illuminate and conceptualize this identifying system that can become imprisoning. I also believe that it is not much more necessary to comment on this rich dream that Iris gave me at the end of her analysis, when I had the good fortune to see her removing the curtain of hair that covered her face, leaving the dark world in which she had taken refuge in search of being somebody, and gradually reconstructing an image of herself based on her most creative potential, although the polysemy of this symbolic production may still suggest much expansion of its meaning. For example, once the confusion with the cruel object was gone, and therefore she would no longer be ruled by the "big boss," she could define her own destiny based on the desires of her true self. I just had to resist the pressures of being me, the "big boss" and lead her through my "analytical mazes." In our relational field, I had to create with her several "clay representations" to help her emerge from the underground where she had been trapped.

Note

1 Psychoanalyst, Full Member and Training Analyst of the Porto Alegre Psycho-analytical Association.

Bibliographical references

Aisenstein, M. (2009) Les exigeances de la representation. Rapport du XXX Con-grés de langue fraçaise.

Botella, C. e S. (2002) *Irrepresentável: Mais além da representação*. Porto Alegre, Socie-dade de Psicologia. Criação Humana, 2002.

Cahn, R. (1999) *O adolescente na psicanálise – a aventura da subjetivação*. Rio de Ja-neiro. Companhia de Freud.

Cassirer, E. (1944) *Ensaio Sobre o Homem*. Ed. Martins Fontes. São Paulo, 1997.

Castoriades-Auglanier, P. (1975) *La violencia de la interpretación: del pictograma al enunciado*. Buenos Aires, Amorrortu, 2004.

Freud, S. (1911) – Formulações sobre os dois princípios do funcionamento mental. Obras psicológicas completas de Sigmund Freud. Editora Imago, 2006

Levy, Ruggero (1996) "Refúgios narcisistas na adolescência: entre a busca de pro-teção e o risco de destruição – dilemas na contratransferência." *Revista Brasileira de Psicanálise*, 30(1), 1–18.

Levy, Ruggero (2001) "Do símbolo à simbolização." Paper for Membro Efetivo da Sociedade Psicanalítica de Porto Alegre, presented in January 2001.

Levy, R. (2022) « L'objet, l'autre – le choix de l'objet à l'adolescence. » *Rev Fr Psycha-nal* 86(5): 1097–1104.

Meltzer, D. (1973) *Os Estados Sexuais da Mente*. Ed. Imago, Rio de Janeiro, 1979.

Marty, P. (1990) *La psicosomática del adulto*. Amorrortu Editora, Buenos Aires, 2003.

Marty, P. (1992) "Mentalización y psicosomática." Rev. Psicoanálisis. N° 3, p. 7–21.

Meltzer, D. (1966) – "The relation of anal masturbation to projective identification". *International Journal of Psycho-Analysis*, 47: 335–342.

Meltzer, D. (1973) *Os Estados Sexuais da Mente*. Ed. Imago, Rio de Janeiro, 1979.

Meltzer, D. (1978) Seminários de Novara. *Quaderni di Psicoterapia Infantile*. Roma, Bokla.

Meltzer, D. (1988) *A Apreensão do Belo*. Imago Editora. Rio de Janeiro, 1995.

Meltzer, D. (1992) *The Claustrum – An Investigation of Claustrophobic Phenomena*. The Clunie Press for The Roland Harris Trust Library.

Ogden, T. (1994) *Os sujeitos da Psicanálise*. São Paulo. Casa do Psicólogo, 1996.

Winnicott, D. W. (1951) "Objetos transicionais e fenômenos transicionais." In: *O Brincar e a Realidade*. Imago Editora. Rio de Janeiro, 1975.

Winnicott, D. W. (1967) "O papel da mãe e da família no desenvolvimento emocional infantil." In: *O Brincar e a Realidade*. Imago Editora. Rio de Janeiro, 1975.

6 Psychoanalytic atmosphere
Struggles between intimacy and respect

Clara Nemas

Introduction

It is not easy to pinpoint the moment in which one has become a psychoanalyst. Like in other aspects of life, we are always becoming. As Freud said, "there is much more continuity between intra-uterine life and earliest infancy than the impressive caesura of the act of birth allows us to suppose" (Freud 1926:138).

Nevertheless, there are particular moments in our life which from a psychoanalytic perspective, following Bion, we may regard as catastrophic changes, or moments in the path of personality development in Meltzer's terms. In a poetic language, Murakami calls them sandstorms.

> *And once the storm is over you won't remember how you made it through, how you managed to survive. You won't even be sure, in fact, whether the storm is really over. But one thing is certain. When you come out of the storm you won't be the same person who walked in. That's what this storm's all about."*
>
> (Murakami 2002)

These sandstorms keep happening and changing directions all through our lives, but unlike Murakami, who thinks that when the storm is over we will not be the same person who walked in, I believe they are part of a process of transformation in which "*something* has remained unaltered and on this *something* recognition depends. The elements that go to make up the unaltered aspect of the transformation I shall call invariants" (Bion 1965:1).

> *Sometimes fate is like a small sandstorm that keeps changing directions. You change direction but the sandstorm chases you. You turn again, but the storm adjusts.*
>
> (Murakami 2002)

Thinking about the stormy times we live in, paraphrasing Meltzer (1992), *in this still primitive century, not very far after the caves as it were*, we had to

DOI: 10.4324/9781003441861-7

turn and adjust once and again in our psychoanalytic world in ways that had not been foreseeable.

In the epigraph above, I quoted the Wolf Man in his recollections as *less as a patient than as a co-worker,* of Sigmund Freud in his analysis with him (Gardiner, 1972). I used this quotation in my paper *Development is Beauty, Growth is Ethics* (2000) and it has stayed with me over the years as a description of the ethical position of Freud in his work as a psychoanalyst. I don't know of any account of a patient of Meltzer about his/her analysis, but I can tell about the way it felt being in supervision with him.

Looking back I think that the contact with the way of Meltzer's thinking and practising psychoanalysis was a moment of caesura. I had teachers, analysts, and supervisors who also made such an impact on me, but meeting him in person, was a very particular experience. There is an anecdote from one of the visits of Meltzer to Brazil related by a colleague (Calich 2004) that transmits something of his openness to emotional contact and disposition. Going out of the airport Meltzer was approached by a psychotic man in tatters. The colleagues welcoming Meltzer tried to keep him away, but Meltzer stopped them and said: "this man has something to say; let's listen to him". The man spoke Portuguese, a language Meltzer did not understand but all the same he listened to this man – to this man's internal objects– in a kind and attentive way. In the end the man went away but before he extended his hand which Meltzer took between his two hands and they each one said, in their own language that it had been a pleasure to meet the other. Meltzer commented: this man is very confused but has good internal objects; he has a lot to tell if anybody would listen to him. The man said: take care of him; he is a very wise person! I think this is a very good example of the intimate atmosphere Meltzer was capable of creating in different circumstances.

Almost 50 years ago, in the early seventies, I participated in a seminar at the Tavistock Clinic dictated by Donald Meltzer. The subject was Freud's clinical cases; something that long after I recognized as the First Volume of The Kleinian Development (Meltzer 1978). We were a group of young students sitting in circle. It was a lively conversation between students and teacher in an atmosphere of freedom to make comments and ask questions. Besides the subject discussed, there were other questions that uncovered curiosity about what psychoanalysis was about. One particular question sounded naive, but the reply Meltzer gave was illuminating. One student asked why it was not convenient to talk with others about one's analytic sessions. Meltzer replied that it had to do with *intimacy*. He added that it depended on the culture, as in some societies people were very open about their sessions and commented about them in cafes, until they discovered in their analysis the intimacy of the nuptial chamber and started to care about the privacy of their analysis.

Years later Meltzer (1988) expanded this idea including Bion's ideas on symbol formation:

The place of this creative intercourse, so prosaically called the parental bed-room, is the locus of awe and wonder in the internal world. Or more correctly, here is where the alpha function takes place, where the creative act of symbol formation quietly proceeds through the night.

(Meltzer 1988:83)

The way in which Donald Meltzer practised and transmitted psychoanalysis promoted a particular quality, defined by him as that space between temperature and distance which allows the development for an intimate and at the same time respectful link between analyst and patient. We may also add the link between supervisor and supervisee that I have been able to experience in working with him.

For Meltzer, the atmosphere generated in the sessions is composed by a benevolent perspective together with a kind sense of humor that will provide the necessary distance and temperature for a musical dialogue to unfold.

It is in this particular emotional atmosphere – which does not leave out the storms generated in the encounter of two minds to which I will refer later – that Meltzer promotes the growth of buds of symbol formation which are at the core of his interest and of his way of understanding what psychoanalysis has to offer. (Nemas, 2008)

Psychoanalytic atmosphere is related to and is at the same time different from psychoanalytic attitude. The analytic attitude refers to that aspect of the psychoanalytic situation, by means of which the patient's need for objects of transference can find a realization in the figure of the analyst. In one of his last papers, Bion (1979) said that 'when two personalities meet, an emotional storm is created' and psychotherapy can only ever aim to 'make the best of a bad job' by turning that storm between the two people in the room to good account. Some years earlier, in 1971, in his book *Sincerity, a study in the atmosphere of human relations*, Meltzer made a remarkable description of the storms psychoanalysis may and does start off.

> ... one is left aghast at the temerity of the psychoanalytic method, which dares to throw two strangers together in the expectation of their having a thousand or so hours of intimate, spontaneous, emotional conversation, not to mention therapeutic benefit to patient and scientific or technical advance for the analyst.

But this does not relate only to the scientific growth of the analyst. He further adds: "And the wonder of it is that they eventually achieve a dialogue of endless interest, which must finally be relinquished by both of them, for the same reason as it is necessary for the mother to wean the baby" (Meltzer 1971:280).

It is this "...endless interesting conversation" which makes the infantile transference to become possible. In a poetic language, Meltzer describes the infantile as the innate equipment standing in relation to the self as the natural resources of a country stand in relation to the human community or, using another analogy, as the total physical environment, given by nature and history, stands in relation to the new generations (Meltzer, 1976).

I think of the infantile as an arrow that traverses all mental states at every moment of our lives. We give meaning and we try to understand the world from our original helplessness, vividly described by Melanie Klein (1937), from a paradoxical situation by which as human beings, we are so dependent on our objects but at the same time we are alone.

It is in this space between dependence and loneliness where intimacy develops. The psychoanalytic session is perhaps one of the only intimate places left in these times in which the need to be "liked" in social media pays the price: the private lives of people become public and are exposed to scrutiny and cruel cancelation. We are bombarded by a world of images where the boundaries between what is private, intimate and public have been blurred. What is considered private and public or the value given to both, vary through history, they are sociological constructions.

Intimacy is a more complex and difficult concept to define as it includes aspects which may appear as contradictory. On the one hand, it refers to the most inner aspect of oneself, one that is never shared; but, on the other hand, it also refers to the closest relationship we can have with another person. Following Francoise Jullien, intimacy signifies *my* most inward part, *my* intimate conviction, and as soon as I verbalize this there must be the presence of *the other* (Jullien 2013). In this sense, intimacy gives rise to *we*; the very source of intimacy is the in-between, in other words, intimacy is the relationship itself.

Meltzer differentiates interactions from relationships; one of his main concerns was to … *"distinguish phenomena in our patients and ourselves which are the consequences of emotional experiences which have been subjected to symbol formation, thought, judgement, decision, and possible transformation into language, from others which are habitual, automatic, and unintentional"* (Meltzer 1986:21).

Following Bion, who described an external carapace and an inner skeleton in all personalities, Meltzer refers to an outward armory directed toward the contractual and casual world, and an inner structure related to internal objects and infantile parts of the personality, which are also closely connected with intimate relationships, the private world, and the private life. The carapace or exoskeleton of the personality is directed outward as an adaptation shell, whose intention is survival and prospering.

In 1986, he proposes that: *The term "intimate" human relationships… is the realm I wish to reserve for the emotional experiences that set thought in motion. For convenience I might contrast them with areas of interaction that are so casual as to involve no emotion, or so contractual as to preclude spontaneous emotional response* (Meltzer 1986:27).

In Meltzer's conception of the psychoanalytic process there is as a path of transformation from contractual interactions expressed in the pre-formed transference, (Meltzer 1967:7) to the development of emotionally meaningful experiences that set thought in motion. In other words, the psychoanalytic process puts in motion and promotes a process of emotional experience and learning, being the primary task to enable the development of an imaginative construction of a picture of the world which includes new ideas and precludes omniscience. This perspective of psychoanalysis is inspired by Bion's ideas on the centrality of emotions in the development of the mind and the personality, focusing attention on the central importance of emotions in mental life and of aesthetic experience as the model of what truly happens in analysis.

An emotional experience is an encounter with the beauty and mystery of the world which arouses conflict between L, H and K, and minus L, H and K. While the immediate meaning is experienced as emotion, maybe as diverse as the objects of immediate arousal, its significance is always ultimately concerned with intimate human relationships.

(Meltzer 1986:26)

This is a conception of psychoanalysis as an aesthetic and ethical object for analyst and patient. As I proposed in a paper mentioned above *Development is Beauty, Growth is Ethics* (Nemas 2000)... "the aesthetic conflict implies a change in paradigm in the sense that conflict in relation to the present object is prior in significance to anxieties with regard to the absent object". In other words, I would now say that the main source of anxiety is related to the need to tolerate the presence of the psychic reality, the unknown interior of the object which we wish not only to discover and to know but also to intrude and to control.

The background of this conception of psychoanalysis lies in Melanie Klein's discovery of the fact that we live in more than one world at the same time and that we inhabit our internal world in a very concrete way. The meaning of the world emanates from our internal landscape in a constant flux between introjection and projection. Let´s think of an image of a beach, the ocean on one side, the dry sand on the other and in the middle a stretch of wet sand. This is how I imagine the internal world as a constant coming and going of the tide and the waves that create something new, not liquid and not solid, not totally underwater and not dry, full of myriads of tiny holes that disappear under a bubble in no time stirring up our curiosity.

Freud broadened our understanding of the working of the mind with his description of psychic reality. This concept gave a new dimension to what we understand not only as real, but also about what is true. Melanie Klein went even further by describing an internal world we inhabit (Klein

1940); she talks of the conception of the infant about the interior of the mother's body and as a consequence of the baby's own interiority. Klein described this internal world as a theatre stage with characters on it: a stage populated by internal objects and parts of the self in close and at the same time fantastic and distorted relation to each other and to the self.

This spatial view of mental life which is central to the Kleinian tradition has been developed by Meltzer in his understanding of the geography of the mind as an addendum to metapsychology (Bianchedi et al. 1984). The desire to penetrate the barriers surrounding these worlds – private, public, and secret – may be taken as driving forces toward intimacy, on the one hand, and violence on the other.

In *The Problem of Violence* (1988), Meltzer remarks that each individual "makes his daily round with an atmosphere whose boundaries threaten repellent if trespassed". ... "For this is the essential meaning of private/secret: that entry must be invited". What he means is that every trespassing of boundaries are not only violent but may be considered as a violation; a violation of internal boundaries.

Struggles with intimacy and respect

Intimacy relates to the link between objects that may stir up emotions which not always are tolerable. I mentioned above that the main source of anxiety is related to the need to tolerate the presence of the psychic reality of the object. The experience of envy depends on the awareness of separateness, an experience of the otherness of the other as the not me; the reservoir of all the good that I do not possess.

In the famous painting of the Sistine Chapel by Michelangelo, *The Birth of Adam*, Adam is facing God the father enclosed in a red mantel–the interior of the mother with the internal babies? – He is surrounded by angels and by the figure of a woman. The fingers of Adam and God are close but they do not touch; there is a gap between them that has been often commented about. Would that gap between closeness and separation point to that serene and at the same time intense space between intimacy and isolation, between closeness and separation that we intent to describe with the words intimacy and respect?

In her book on envy Melanie Klein (1957) explores the relation of the infant to his/her first object – the mother's breast and the mother – ... "*I have drawn the conclusion that if the primal object, which is introjected, takes root in the ego with relative security, the basis for a satisfactory development is laid.*" (Klein 1957:178). The intimacy between mother and baby is passionate and intense but by no way serene. The circumstances of birth, postpartum depression in the mother, the strain on the baby to tolerate the aesthetic impact of the world without falling apart, and the capacity for reciprocity in the aesthetic impact of mother and baby, influence the quality of intimacy that may develop in the relationship.

The conceptualization of envy by Melanie Klein (1957) introduced the need to recognize *that the conflict about the present object is prior in significance to the host of anxieties over the absent object* (Meltzer 1988:29). The understanding of envy as related to an intolerable awareness of a separate object in possession of inexhaustible good but idealized qualities, relegated to a secondary place the idea of mental pain originating by external frustration. The whole description of the aesthetic conflict derives from this awareness about the passionate reaction to the outside of the "beautiful" must be construed by imagination. The uncertainty about the mind of the mother may become intolerable; when that happens intrusiveness is felt as the only recourse available in order to escape from the mystery of the unknown.

The idea of the link, of a linking function that connects human beings and our vicissitudes, is one of Bion's major contributions to our way of thinking, understanding, and working with our patients and with ourselves. In this realm, reverie is a mysterious – and not always present – emotional state that underlines and illuminates object relations and the birth of the psyche from the beginning of life. This function describes, in the best of cases, a natural capacity in the mind of the mother that allows her to accept, to lodge within herself, and then transform the baby's primitive nonverbal communications into alpha elements, gradually helping the baby become capable of thinking thoughts and feeling feelings. The most important outcome of this process is the introjection by the baby of this maternal capacity. This introjected maternal capacity promotes the baby's – incipient – capacity to tolerate his or her own psychic qualities; in other words, it allows us to be able to own our emotional states without (much) denial or projection (Nemas 2016).

When this process is interfered by the mother or the baby, the atmosphere of the relationship with the mother shifts from accepting the mystery of her interior to solving the enigma, violating boundaries and penetrating by projective identification the opaque space of the interior of the object. Intimacy is necessary forth emotional and mental growth in the development of human beings. In the struggle between developmental and anti-developmental forces alluded at in the delineation of the *negative grid*, -K, -L, -K, there is a constant threat to the establishment of intimate loving bonding.

> *In the struggle against the negative links this capacity to tolerate uncertainty, not knowing, the "cloud of unknowing" is constantly called upon in the passion of the intimate relations and is at the heart of the matter of aesthetic conflict.*

> (Meltzer 1988:20)

This struggle lies at the core of the psychoanalytic process; to include this perspective gives new meaning to negative transference associated with hostility and lacking in trust, with the counterpart of incomprehension and confusion in the counter transference. In his lecture on negative transference, Meltzer (2017a) relates hostility and even contempt for the analyst and the resulting counter-transference of incomprehension and confusion, to lack of imaginative capacity; a capacity to conceive what lays hidden in the object, and to observe the inner sense of things. Something I related in other paper to the capacity to develop imaginable conjectures, to which I shall refer related to in a vignette bellow (Nemas 2017).

These ideas enrich the meaning of what many years ago we heard him say at his lecture to the Therapy Group in London, in which he spoke of being more concerned about what the mind does well than about what it does wrong, more concerned with the depressive position than with the schizoid-paranoid position. At that time, these comments stirred some technical questions about the interpretation of negative transference. In a lecture given in Venice to the Racker Group, Meltzer clarifies further his understanding of negative transference in a way that changes the conception of the way we inhabit the psychoanalytic atmosphere of our work.

> *The patient's inability is one of failing to understand the nature of positive relations, the true significance behind words like love, hate, knowledge; he is unable to understand their true meaning; to him they are just words without significance; he does not know what it means to love, hate or be interested in others.*
>
> (Meltzer 2017a:234)

The clinical expression of this shallowness, according to Meltzer, is a sense of boredom felt by both the therapist toward the patient, and the patient toward the analyst. What is interesting is what can be analyzed underneath this boredom; mainly the lack of interest – K link–that causes it.

I consider that this turn in the understanding of psychoanalytic atmosphere is influenced by Money-Kyrle's concept of "misconception"[1] included in his theory of "cognitive development" that Meltzer considers a "new idea with considerable descriptive powers that other theories do not possess"(Meltzer 1971:497).

> *What actually happens is that, while part of the developing personality does learn to understand the facts of life, suffers the pains of the Oedipus complex, discards it from guilt, becomes reconciled to the parental relation, internalizes it and achieves maturity, other parts remain ignorant and retarded.*
>
> (Money-Kyrle 1978:693)

In Meg Williams account of a joint seminar given on Interpretation versus Interpretative Reverie, by Martha Harris and Donald Meltzer at the Novara Seminars in the early seventies, Meg Williams reports Meltzer's position on negative aspects in the process: "a negative therapeutic reaction" is often the result of the way an interpretation is given: in the form of a judgement, rather than thinking aloud in company with the patient (Meltzer 2021:130).

Meltzer felt that the special charm of the concept of misconception is its non-judgmental quality while not ignoring the role of evil in conflict with good in regards to internal processes.

Is the aspect of respect present in the psychoanalytic atmosphere included in the ethical concept of neutrality in the analyst? Neutrality is a concept that has given way to numerous discussions and elaboration among analysts from different perspectives.

In his article *Lines of Advance in Psycho-Analytic Therapy*, Freud says:

> *We refused most emphatically to turn a patient who puts himself into our hands in search of help into our private property, to decide his fate for him, to force our own ideals upon him, and with the pride of a Creator to form him in our own image and see that is good ... I have been able to help people with whom I had nothing in common – neither race, education, social position nor outlook upon life in general – without affecting their individuality.*
>
> (Freud 1919:164–165)

We might ask who is the subject that put on us a pressure we must refuse to comply to. We know that at the time, Freud was discussing active methods in psychoanalysis, but we may add that anti-developmental forces in the patient may also put pressure on the analyst to divert him/her from a psychoanalytic attitude. Another serious obstacle to psychoanalytic attitude or what we address today as respect in the psychoanalytic atmosphere are, on the side of the analyst according to Melanie Klein, the appearance of "feelings of power and superiority" (Klein 2017:31).

> *A fundamental respect for the working of the mind and for human nature, which is implicit in all real insight into its laws and economy, also implies a true sensation of our own limitations, and yet at the same time is the only foundation for a true belief in the curative power of psychoanalysis.*
>
> (Klein 2017:31)

Meltzer emphasizes observation as the core feature of psychoanalytic work; observation and the development of a capacity to describe the world the patient lives in derived precisely from observation. It involves the task of conceptualizing the world in which there is a conception of the internal family and they exist as a member of the family.

> "... our work ... is one of observing ... and in a sense, not meddling. We can be astronomers without sending a man to the moon..."
>
> (Meltzer 2017b:212)

Some reflections on clinical work

As I mentioned above, in a lecture Meltzer gave in 1989 to the Therapy Group in London, he said something quite remarkable which has remained quite present and alive in my mind since then. I recall it more or less as follows:

> At this time in my work I am more concerned with nurturing and assisting the buds of the mind that are capable of thinking than with clearing out the weeds; that is, more interested in what the mind does well than in what it does badly or, in other words, less inclined to place the accent on the functioning of the paranoid-schizoid than on the depressive position.

This position about the emphasis in the interpretations more directed toward the depressive than to the paranoid/schizoid positions seemed to express a change in the conception of the analytic task, fruit of his interaction with ideas of Bion. Meltzer considered that psychoanalysis is halfway between child-raising and family life and it is likely that his progressively waning interest in psychopathology is associated with this perspective on analytic work. The function of the family, the family that is presided by the couple and analysis related to family life, carry the functions of generating love, promoting hope, containing depressive pain, and thinking.

The objective of psychoanalysis in this line of work, based on Bion's ideas, evolved from a medical model – in which someone helped another person who was suffering from mental and emotional difficulties to resolve a conflict – to a family model in which patient and analyst experience the transference and countertransference together, analogous to – though by no means identical – to the relation between parents and their small children. This way of conceiving analytic work is a hallmark of Meltzer's way of thinking, and I believe it has strongly influenced the people who have been in contact with his ideas.

Returning to Bion: as we said, the shift in the way of conceiving of the analytic process brought about further change: from the objective of *curing* – associated with the medical model – toward the concept of *evolution*. This evolution is not linear; it implies just the opposite: mental growth and retraction as processes that, as in a spiral, follow one another in the analysis. The result of these processes is determined by the degree of tolerance and ability to think about the emotional turbulence – *catastrophic changes* – (Bion 1970) in the relationship between analyst and patient, so that they become mental growth rather than catastrophe.

What Bion termed *catastrophic change* becomes *development* of the personality in Meltzer. This kind of development may at times place everything at risk, which in a former paper I related to the courage to analyze and be analyzed. Unlike the horticultural model proposed by Klein, according to

Meltzer, in which given good conditions the personality develops more or less linearly, from the meltzerian perspective the development of the personality is characterized by constant revolution, albeit a private revolution, and is even *invisible to the eyes*, as tends to occur with *the essential*, in the words of *The Little Prince*. The elements of this revolution are sincerity, passionate support of emotional ties and the ability to confront changes.

Clinical vignettes

A girl called 4 years old

A young patient complains that she feels she has two parts regarding her feelings toward her partner. On the one hand, she likes the fact that they are both autonomous, she likes having time on her own, not to have to share everything with her girlfriend but when the girlfriend goes to a party without her, she feels jealous and possessive and she would like to make that feeling disappear from her mind. She feels that the two parts fight with each other to see which one gets the upper hand. She defines one aspect as rational and the other as irrational. How do other people manage with this kind of feelings? She spoke to a friend who told her that he never felt this way; she does not want to look down on him but she actually thinks that he dealt with his feelings by becoming a drug addict. Each person is different – she says – and takes things in a different way. I told her that even if she does not want to despise her friend, she seems ready to despise her own feelings. She looked surprised but agreed. Then I proposed that instead of talking of rational or irrational we tried to date those two aspects of her, to give them an age. She did not understand what I meant, so I said: suppose the one you call irrational is 4 years old and the rational is 28. She protested as if the intention of my interpretation would have been to take her back to the time when she was a child of 8 years of age, when the family moved to B.A. We both knew how disruptive that time had been for her. I said that she understood that I was referring to her history and not to a 4 years old conception of the world as she seemed to prefer to take what I said as related to her actual childhood. I mentioned something about that somehow talking about the infantile seemed derogative. She replied that she actually liked the infantile in people and in herself. I said that it seemed that she liked it as long as it was something related to creativity and the capacity to play, not to these other lesser aspects of the personality. Later in the session, I added that the capacity to feel jealousy derived from the capacity to imagine the other person in a situation when the other is not with the child and is somewhere else. I added later that even the capacity to distrust was an evidence of the recognition of the opacity of the other person, the evidence of the incapacity to know everything about the other. (At that moment I remembered my youngest grandchild; when asked what would be the superpowers she would like to have, she replied: to fly and to be invisible!) In the session, a more benevolent atmosphere seemed gradually to appear, less judgmental and less harsh. It felt more playful and she ended telling me how she had been able to rescue a little bird which fell from the nest by feeding it with sugary water until it was strong enough to fly.

The thumb in the mouth – On a supervision of a child analysis

I shall present the supervision of an 11 years old patient whom I will call Ana who had been in analysis for five years when the supervisee presented the case to me. The treatment started when Ana was 6 years old, at the time when her parents were in the middle of a turbulent divorce; the school suggested the consultation. The patient was a first-class student who also excelled in sport and art, but her communication was impeded by her persistent thumb-sucking, which had already provoked a degree of malformation in her palate and teeth. From the beginning, her face showed no emotion and she wore a fixed smile. In her sessions, she built elaborate constructions and small-scale models that she kept tidily in her box, together with the strips of paper she had used to make them.

Years passed before Ana showed any emotion in the sessions; she could cry and express feelings of anger and frustration, but her thumb remained in her mouth, despite continued efforts to understand this fixed symptom.

After some supervisions in which we discussed the analyst's interventions and Ana's response to them, I proposed to the supervisee to talk to the thumb-in-the-mouth as if it were another character in the session. How did the thumb feel inside the mouth, and how did it think it might feel if it went outside the mouth? Was it scared to leave its sanctuary? Was it curious about what went on outside? Would it be able to get back inside if it felt too scared outside? All of a sudden all these questions started coming up, in a way that in the supervision we could empathize with the fear of the thumb getting out of its refuge as a personification of the unborn baby part of the personality, which did not dare come out into the world. This was not verbalized in an interpretation to the patient.

The analyst started playing a play role game in the sessions, and it took some time for the girl to engage in it. The therapist would personify the finger, talking in the first person, and Ana would speak for the other characters in the mouth: the teeth, tongue, and lips. Sometimes they changed roles. They started making up stories in the session about the thumb who had been adopted by this mouth family. Mostly, the thumb felt safe but sometimes it felt threatened by foreign things coming in, by the moving tongue or the biting teeth.

The thumb-in-the-mouth became a subject of shared interest between analyst and patient. The thumb-in-the-mouth worked as shorthand between analyst and patient. It stood as a part of the personality of the patient in the manner described by Melanie Klein in her wonderful text

Personification in the Play of Children (1929). The repetitive action of building small-scale models tidily preserved was replaced by a renewed mutual interest as a more creative imagination started taking place in the sessions around the story of the-thumb-in-the-mouth. I understand this evolution as the development of what I have called *imaginable conjectures;* this refers to the possibility of opening up of unknown and un-thought of spaces in the mind in which something new can take place, not only challenging established theories, but giving place to the possibility that new theories and conjectures may develop in a still unexplored territory (Nemas 2017).

Buds of positive feelings

A patient enumerates in detail the attacks she feels she receives from different people related to (because) of her pregnancy, but mentions that she is surprised that she hasn't received any aggression from her mom, as she might have expected. Quite the opposite, she is tender and kind, something that on other occasions was precisely what triggered the patient's rejection and irritability toward the mother.

She quoted her mother saying: "You were sucking the breast and saying 'goo-goo' and now you're pregnant!" She has even considered that she might at some time leave her baby in her mother's care, since she watched her while she was looking after her little niece and both were playing in a serene atmosphere. I interpreted that her little niece probably represented a baby aspect of herself that can let itself be looked after, because it accepts being mommy's baby. At another moment in the session, she commented that she was afraid that her mother, who knows me professionally, might say something bad about me. Her comments had usually been appreciative, she all the same was afraid that she might say something negative. In the context of this session, I interpreted that perhaps her anxiety that her mother might say something inconvenient was because she now feels more trusting of me and can tolerate negative comments about me.

The interpretation of the projection of her own criticism toward the analyst into the fear that her mother might make a negative comment would of course not be far from the material, but it might risk drowning the budding positive feelings in conflict with the hostility.

Accepting clinical material as food

Another patient, who had immovable complaints about her parents, comments in a session that, after observing tantrum in the daughter of a friend of hers, she thought that she too must have been an 'unbearable' little girl when she was small. She narrates a dream in which someone gives her a tray with toy food: dough, marzipan, studded balls like in the Middle Ages, ropes with knots like the Indians make, but all made of paste and served like pastries in a tea shop. She associates with the desserts her mother used to make and with her sister's girlfriends who ate them voraciously. She goes on, talking about her boyfriend and her wish to shine out that induces him to compete with her, and about a time when she felt very hurt by a comment of his regarding his impression of how careless she would be with a baby.

The possibility to talk about having been – and of still being – a little girl hard to 'endure', without feeling rejected and criticized, was a new material. The interpretation was aimed at her expectation that I would be able to recognize new food. This new food referred both to her possibility of thinking about herself as a little girl – and as a patient – in a new light, and also to conceive of analytic work as something different from a competition between us to be the brighter star. This involves recognizing that if the interpretation can be food, so is the material that she offers.

The ethics of technique – the working atmosphere

In relation to our task as psychoanalysts, I would like to include a final point in this presentation: the ethics of technique in Meltzer (Nemas 2000). Meltzer thinks that the psychoanalytic method has – and acquires for some of his patients – an aesthetic quality.

In her article *Personification in the Play of Children* (1929), Melanie Klein said "… that the analyst must simply be a medium in relation to whom the different imagos can be activated and the phantasies lived through, in order to be analyzed" (Klein 1929:209). This is quite a modest position with respect to the analyst's role in the transference, to which Meltzer adds a dimension: he proposes that the transference object is not the analyst himself or herself, but rather the analyst's internal objects, which the analyst shares with his or her patients. The analyst's relation with his or her own internal objects is the origin of intuition for understanding the patient; in this sense, something about the atmosphere in the room, as I said before, is very similar to the upbringing of children in family life.

The container-contained model that Bion contributes (Bion 1963) is used by Meltzer to describe the analytic situation. Sometimes, with some patients, the entire analysis must be contained for a time in the analyst's mind, but in a developing psychoanalytic process the container is formed by the analyst's attentive receptiveness and the patient's cooperativeness. This shared responsibility for the analytic task transforms the relationship between analyst and patient into a work group of two, operating in a non-authoritarian atmosphere in which each does his or her job according to their capabilities. The function of understanding, divested of the expectation of knowing, allows for greater freedom to speculate and opens up a path to the development of creative imagination.

The analyst's aspiration is not to increase knowledge, but to resolve confusions in development, to clarify forms of dependence toward the good object and to explore narcissistic aspects of the personality that interfere in the intimacy of the contact between the baby and the good object.

The qualities of the good objects in the internal world engender trust in justice and in the parent's availability to infantile aspects in the self. This contact with the parental couple enable tolerance and modulation of the pain inherent to emotional life, in the hope to stimulate the interest – K link – to explore both motivations and consequences throughout the inevitable emotional storms of the development of the personality.

To conclude

In that lecture given in 1989, Meltzer said that when he first went to London to undergo analysis with Melanie Klein, he found in the maps of the city places marked in greenmarked as POP: "permanent open spaces". I would like to end this contribution quoting Meltzer in an unfinished paper he wrote in 2002 as a newspaper report, titled *Adolescence: after the hurricane*, which takes us back to Murakami sandstorms. I chose to end this contribution with this quotation as I find that the quality of unfinished is a metaphor for those permanent open spaces in which to continue developing his seminal ideas.

> *The analytic situation is…* "*the development of an honest and sincere cooperation between two partners of the analytic setting, permitting them to ignore hearsay, gossip, and various beliefs which claim to be reasonable.*" *Instead there is the deep conviction that, he said,* "*the ultimate criterion of true reasonableness is a labour of love, and it results in the achievement of beauty – in its ultimate form, poetry.*" (Meltzer, 2017b, pp. xxi–xxii)

Note

1 "… the patient, whether clinically ill or not, suffers from unconscious misconceptions and delusions… My aim has been to outline a theory of this interaction (between our perception of truth and the will to distort it)" (Money-Kyrle, 1978, p. 417).

References

Bianchedi, E., et al. (1984). Beyond Freudian Metapsychology, *The International Journal of Psychoanalysis*, 65, 389.

Bion, W. R. (1963). Elements of Psychoanalysis, London: Karnal books, 1984.

Bion, W. R. (1965). *Transformations*, London: Karnac Books, 1984.

Bion, W. R. (1970). *Attention and Interpretation.* Tavistock; reprinted Karnak 1984.

Bion, W. R. (1979). Making the best of a bad job. In: F. Bion (Ed.), *Clinical Seminars and Four Papers*. London: Karnac, 1987.

Calich, J. C. (2004). *Meltzer en persona: unimpactoestético*, Revista de Psicoanálisis de la Sociedad Psicoanalítica de Porto Alegre (SPPA), 429–435, Vol. XI – N°3.

Freud, S. (1919). *Introductory Lectures on Psycho-Analysis*, Vol. XVI, The Standard Edition. London: The Hogarth Press, 1928.

Freud, S. (1926). *Inhibition, Symptom and Anxiety*, Vol. XX, The Standard Edition. London: The Hogarth Press.

Gardiner, M. (1972). *The Wolf-Man and Sigmund Freud*, Great Britain: Penguin Books, 1973.

Jullien, F. (2013). *De l'intime. Far from Noisy Love*, Paris: Grasset. Critical note published in: Dialogue, Toulouse, n° 202, pp. 99–101.

Klein, M. (1929). Personification in the Play of Children. In: *Love, Guilt and Reparation and Other Works*, ed. by R. Money-Kyrle. London: The Hogarth Press, 1981.

Klein, M. (1937). *Love, Guilt and Reparation and Other Works*, London: The Hogarth Press, 1981.

Klein, M. (1940). Mourning and its Relation to Manic-Depressive States. In: *Love, Guilt and Reparation and Other Works*, ed. by R. Money-Kyrle. London: The Hogarth Press, 1981.

Klein, M. (1957). *Envy and Gratitude and Other Works*, London: The Hogarth Press, 1980.

Klein, M. *Lectures on Technique by Melanie Klein*. Edited by John Steiner, Routledge. 2017.

Meltzer, D. (1967). *The Psycho–Analytical Process*. Scotland:Clunie Press.

Meltzer, D. (1971). *Sincerity and Other Works*, London: Karnac Books, 1994.

Meltzer, D. (1976). A Psychoanalytic Model of the Child-in-the-Family-in-the-Community. In: *Sincerity and Other Works*, Chapter 22, ed. by A. Hahn. London: Karnac Books, 1994.

Meltzer, D. (1978). *The Kleinian Development*, Part I: Freud's Clinical Development, Perthshire: The Clunie Press.

Meltzer, D. (1986). *Studies in Extended Metapsychology*, Scotland: The Clunie Press.

Meltzer, D. (1989). Lecture to the Therapy Group in London. Unpublished.

Meltzer, D. (1992). *The Claustrum: An Investigation of Claustrophobic Phenomena*. Great Britain: The Clunie Press.

Meltzer, D. (2002). *Adolescence: After the Hurricane. A Newspaper Report*. In: *Adolescence: Talks and Papers* by Meltzer and Harris, 2011.

Meltzer, D. (2017a). *Meltzer in Venice*, Seminars with the Racker group of Venice. London: Karnac Books.

Meltzer, D. (2017b). *Meltzer in Paris*. Edited by Jacques Touze, Karnac Books.

Meltzer, D. (2021). *Papers of Donald Meltzer*, Vol. 3 edited by Meg Harris-Williams, London: The Harris Meltzer Trust.

Meltzer, D. and Williams, M.H. (1988). The Problem of Violence. In: *The Apprehension of Beauty*, Scotland: The Clunie Press, p. 83.

Money-Kyrle, R.M. (1978). Cognitive Development. In *The Collected Papers of Roger Money-Kyrle*, ed. by D. Meltzer and E. O'Shaughnessy. Scotland: The Clunie Press.

Murakami, H. (2002). *Kafka on the Shore*, UK: Arrow Editorial, 2006.

Nemas, C. (2000). *Development is Beauty, Growth is Ethics*. Chapter III published in the book Exploring the Work of Donald Meltzer, London: Karnac Books.

Nemas, C. (2008). *Nurturing Buds of Thought More Than Clearing out the Weeds*. Concerning a thought expressed by Donald Meltzer. Presented in "Encontro Internacional: O Pensamento Vivo de Donald Meltzer", San Pablo.

Nemas, C. (2016). Courage and sincerity as a base for reverie and interpretation. Chapter 10 in *From Reverie to Interpretation*, ed. by D. Blue and C. Harrang. London: Karnac.

Nemas, C. (2017). *Imagination as container of potential spaces*. Lecture presented at The 28th Annual Melanie Klein Lecture, Los Angeles.

7 The language of dreams
On symbolism, aesthetics, and interpretation

Elena Ortiz

The symbolic and aesthetics

Throughout his work, Donald Meltzer reviews and recounts for us the influence that the study of the ideas of Sigmund Freud, Melanie Klein, and Wilfred Bion had on him, along with that of the philosophy of language, the Romantic poets, and various conceptions of aesthetics mainly studied with Meg Harris. These sources of inspiration, together with his own originality and imaginative freedom, allowed Meltzer to refine and contribute fundamental theoretical and technical notions related to the analytical work with dreams.

The Kleinian theory of the internal world as a space where a tangible life develops gives dreams a new status. Not only does unconscious fantasy appears as a drama where the internal objects and the self are linked, but additionally this takes place in a perceptible scenario, a specific site with qualities and an atmosphere that are configured according to the relationships it unfolds. Dreams are the vivid staging of fantasies in all their complexity. They certainly imply the realisation and expression of desires, but they also show links, motivations, mechanisms of mental functioning, unconscious narratives, and their emotional consequences.

To this perspective are added insights from the philosophy of language and the keen vision of Bion, who stresses that it is only due to a thinking object that experience can acquire meaning and thus signify the world. Meltzer highlights two central Bionian ideas: emotionality as the centre of thought; and thought understood as an unconscious activity that starts from the internal object. In addition, contemporary philosophical investigations served Meltzer to reposition the hierarchy of emotions.

Previously, meaning was attributed to rational thought and observable facts. The central idea revolved on the premise that everything thought could be enunciated. This position leaves out the field of intuitive knowledge and emotion, relegating the ineffable to the sphere of the mythical, art, or religion. Emotions were deprived of a symbolic, signifying character. Meltzer shows that the beginning of psychoanalytic thinking was influenced by this view.

DOI: 10.4324/9781003441861-8

Developments in language philosophy radically changed the previous perspective and placed symbol formation at the centre: language is deployed primarily to communicate emotional states. This purpose lies at the genesis of speech, which is subsequently used to describe the non-human environment. Also, as philosophy evolves there is a turn whereby meaning is increasingly understood not as an apprehension of external reality but as something generated from within and extended outward.

Goethe created the word "symbol" in the eighteenth century, but it was the contemporary philosophers whom Meltzer studied (Russell, Whitehead, Wittgenstein, Cassirer, Langer) who displayed the most complete and penetrating understanding of the symbolic function. The symbol ceased to be a mere indicating sign for objects and was conceived as a structure that establishes reality itself. It is not arbitrary, like the sign; its meaning cannot be presented by any other means than the symbol itself. In psychoanalysis, Klein and Hanna Segal established a difference between sign and symbol, but before Bion the question of the generation of meaning remained unresolved (Del Palacio, in Ortiz, 2019: 15). Bion claims that, in dreams, the internalised thinking object transforms emotions into dreamlike images, raw material for the construction of thoughts and meanings. The dream is the process par excellence of the construction of meaning; it is a creative activity, an expression and an attempt to resolve emotional conflicts.

> Excluding Bion's work [...] It has not made much progress in investigating thinking or disturbances in thinking, because these functions have their origins at the pre-verbal level. This failure would appear to have its roots in a failure to differentiate between the problems of communication and the problems of thinking
>
> (Meltzer, 1984: 66).

For Bion, the internal object has fundamental functions and attributes that serve the process of development; from this comes the ability to metabolise emotions, think about them, and thus generate a continent space where life acquires meaning. The mental process in which the symbolic function unfolds with the greatest refinement is dreaming. *Dreaming is thinking [...] the creative process of dreaming generates the meaning that can then be deployed to life and relationships in the outside world* (Meltzer, 1984: 46).

Dreams are attempts of the psyche to orient itself towards reality, both internal and external. They are not just puzzles to be decoded, or the result of the fulfilment of wishes or past traumas. They are the authentic and vivid manifestation of the current drama of objects and the *self*; the axis of analytical work (Harris, 1983).

The dream function is the construction of meaning in the internal world. Dreams are the foundation of the way in which life is understood, they are at the base of how a personality is structured and of an optimistic or pessimistic disposition towards the external world. When Meltzer titles one of his most important works *Dream Life,* he emphasises the dynamic, vital, and permanent quality that dreaming implies; it is understood as a *continuum,* with the dream at the centre. While dream life occurs persistently and tacitly, like the digestive process, dreams represent the core point, the centre of the articulation of meanings.

To be in the presence of a dream is to witness a process that is not only expressive but constructive, imprinting meaning on experience. Relationships, the world, identity, events, links with the present, the past or the future; nothing has an intrinsic meaning, it is built from the dream that rests at the heart of mental life. Psychoanalysis offers a vertex and a privileged space to observe these creative levels of the psyche.

There is also an important link between symbolic construction and aesthetics. Kant and the Romantic poets affirm that the point at which the sensible becomes intelligible is primarily aesthetic. Aesthetic judgment is present at the moment of the acquisition of meaning, both with nature and with the artwork (Del Palacio, in Ortiz, 2019: 14).

There are various aesthetic resources contained in the construction of dreams, including plastic figuration. From a Bionian point of view, the mind uses visual images instead of words to create meaning; the image would not be the product of topographical regression (Freud, 1900) but a creative construction charged with meaning in the process of making sense of experience. The function of *reverie* consists essentially in transforming emotions into dreamlike images to construct thoughts (Bion, 1962).

> [...] the "dreaming process has entered the conversation" and entered it as a visual language, often as poignant as a political cartoonist's drawing, which is worth a thousand words
>
> (Meltzer, 1984: 89).

Poetic diction, as well, mainly in the form of metaphor, is involved in the oneiric function. The laws of poetic language influence the organisation of dreams. Meltzer continues the work of a pioneer in thinking about the dream process, Ella Freeman Sharpe (1937), who shows that dreams use lyric resources to achieve their evocative capacity. *The thing about poetry is that it* captures something (Meltzer, 1995: 122). This is Meltzer's way of trying to underline the power of the creation of meaning.

Meltzer thinks that *metaphor is the method 'par excellence' by which the mind operates,* (1984: 87); the symbolic function acquires an aesthetic dimension. In the dream, a transformation takes place from one kind of symbol to another, from verbal to visual language; but far from being impoverished, the resulting construction is enriched by metaphor and other lyrical resources. It is the poetry and the plastic faculties of the dream that capture and give a formal representation to emotional experiences.

The symbolic modalities found in artistic manifestations that *show* are evocative forms different from those that are discursive and merely *say*. The aesthetic theory of dreams that Meltzer proposes distinguishes the limitations of conscious or proto-mental constructions from those that are capable of constructing meanings. This underlines the difference between mental functions that illustrate and capture *versus* the kind of recording proto-mental functioning that is unable to grasp the richness of meanings (Harris, 1983).

In *The Apprehension of Beauty* (1988), Meltzer investigates imagination and the drive towards knowledge (K link, *knowledge*). He argues that the shock of objects that embody an enigma serve as a stimulus and an encouragement for mental development. Meltzer posits that the initial object that triggers this experience is the interior of the mother figure as intuited by the child, but this experience is transferred to other significant objects that surround the individual, as well as to the world at large. The desire for knowledge is linked to mental pain because any object worth knowing escapes the possibility of being apprehended is unknowable in its entirety, and is surrounded by uncertainty.

> Ever since Freud, psychoanalysis has understood the dynamism of the mind as an interplay of conflicting forces such as desire *versus* defence, pleasure *versus* pain, envy *versus* gratitude ... With this thesis, Meltzer proposes a new confrontation within the psyche: emotionality (provoked by the encounter with beauty and truth) against anti-emotionality. The enemy of the forces of development is anti-emotionality, that is, retreating in the face of aesthetic conflict
> (Ortiz, 2023: 76).

Bion, following Keats, named as *negative capability* the mental ability to function in the midst of uncertainties and doubts without resorting to precise reason, an aptitude that implies being able to bear a lack of understanding and knowledge. Meaning, which is the result of the thinking process, would be developed or not according to the mind's capacity to tolerate the complexity and mystery that the object entails. The effort and the desire to know pushes forward the imagination as a way to approach the incomprehensible.

Clinical work and interpretation

Meltzer's clinical work is deeply influenced by his theory of dreams. He encourages the use of metaphorical descriptions in therapy because they open up new meanings. Metaphor, like good dreams, captures contained emotional experience.

José Carlos Calich says that Meltzer, when conducting clinical supervisions, tried to form a *detailed and predominantly visual image of the patient's*

inner world and the analytical relationship ... He thus constructed a visual image
that allowed him to conjecture the plot and drama of the patient's internal objects
within a geography constructed by mental states (Calich, 2022). The observations that Meltzer makes for himself regarding the patient, which will
later be the basis of his interpretative descriptions, can reassemble the
most creative and symbolic modalities he finds in dreams.

In Buenos Aires, in the late 90s, Meltzer supervises Laura, a 17-year-old
patient who is very affected by a family quarrel between her father and a
cousin, a dispute that creates great stife, the rest of the family takes sides,
she is hurt by the distance with the cousin, a daughter of her uncle, and
because many family vacation plans are broken off and cancelled. The girl
makes constant efforts not to create problems, writes letters giving advice,
behaves impeccably but is increasingly silent, isolated, and presents cry-
ing fits.

Meltzer thinks that she has an idealised view of herself and the family, a
grandiose position, and believes that she has suffered a great disappointment because of the family falling apart. He also shows that she struggles to remain in latency and defend herself against sexuality. Meltzer
displays acute theoretical and clinical insights; he shows his perspectives
on the patient's psychopathology and the transference that unfolds with
the analyst. However, the richness of his contributions takes on a special
dimension when they appear transformed into plastic metaphors that are
reminiscent of the language of dreams:

> ... It's a bit like Jesus telling the apostles "Love one another" ... [She
> has an ...] attitude of Christian beatification. It would be a bit like the
> change from baby Jesus with that beatific face on Mary's lap bless-
> ing everyone, to an image of Jesus on the cross taking on the sins of
> mankind. It is essentially a manic-depressive displacement... [In the
> letters she writes she thinks that others should share their problems
> with her...] and she is going to advise them from her infinite wisdom.
> [She feels that she is...] the family's ray of sunshine, and that people
> just need to accept her infinite love and generosity and all problems
> will be solved
>
> (APdeBA, 1999: 179–195).

Meltzer understands the patient-analyst relationship as an aesthetic process of symbol formation (Harris, 2010b). The degree of accuracy in the
content of an interpretation acquires a new value because *the poetic ability*
of the analyst to discover and verbalise the patient's emotional experience
also matters. The goal is to turn the analytical space into a *meeting of minds*
(Meltzer, 1986: 82). The analytical exercise thus departs from a purely in-
tellectual function. The required bond is one where identification with
the patient prevails and the analyst can offer his *imaginative thinking* at the
service of symbolic formation.

Meltzer is also very adept at grasping the patient's position vis-à-vis the analytic method, apprehending the conceptions that the patient has towards the analysis and the analyst, and grasping the *logic of thought established in each objectual plot* (Calich, 2022). Meltzer understands the type of logic/fantasy that structures the configuration of the internal world, as well as the way in which it is expressed in the dynamics of transference.

In Laura's case, Meltzer tells the analyst:

> [...] What the transference implies is obviously that you have great difficulty treating her, and she would like to help you. She can tell you exactly how to improve the situation. First, she must call you by your name. Secondly, you must tell her all your problems, she will advise you and in turn she will tell you her own. You will establish this mutual relationship of love and infinite help, and there will be no more problems
>
> (APdeBA, 1999: 179-195).

The logic of the object plot that unfolds in Laura's universe extends, of course, to the analytical relationship. The transference becomes the axis and the central angle from which to intervene, while the resource of metaphor provides a rich and dynamic instrument to reveal the workings of fantasy now in relation to the analyst.

The metaphorisation of experience

José is a 33-year-old patient who begins analysis due to symptoms of anxiety and periods of depression. Since adolescence he has often compared himself to others and had feelings of inferiority, growing inhibited with women and consuming alcohol. He is estranged from his family due to intense jealousy with his siblings, especially with the youngest brother, but also with his sister, who is currently pregnant. He is angry with their mother for what he considers the excessive support that she gives his sister. Despite having a master's degree and a solid job, he does not feel professionally satisfied. At 22 he began psychotherapy, fell in love with his therapist and eventually abandoned treatment.

During the sessions there is an oscillation in his emotional state. He often wants to impress the analyst, to show her that he has intelligent thoughts, often by using theoretical psychoanalytic language and making pseudo-interpretations. The analyst perceives these seductive attempts as those of a child wishing to catch the mother's attention. At other times José feels resentful, uncared for, unimportant, and depressed.

He constantly dreams that he is running late, cannot arrive where he needs to go, is looking for something and cannot find it.

Here is one of his dreams:

I had to go on a trip, I was going to the airport, and I was the pilot. I was going in the plane, as if it was a car, but something happens, I don't know if there was a blockage or a crash. Suddenly I see the scene in third person, the pilots get off and look defeated, I am left with the feeling that I did not get to where I had to go.

The dream itself is a valuable metaphor for pain and a feeling of failure in trying to position himself in an oedipal place: If José was the actual pilot, he should pilot the plane and assume the most important role in the flight, be ahead of any other crew member or passengers and take control of the ship. The dream begins with him placed in the pilot's aggrandised place and there is a comparison where a car and an airplane are the same.

The representation of the plane as the mother, the pilot as the father and the crew or passengers as siblings is conceivable, as well as the idea that the crash of the plane is the very consequence of the attempted appropriation of this place. The dream seems to be sequential: if you try to usurp the role of the father pilot by equating child and adult, the risk of it ending in failure is high.

When José starts making self-interpretations to try to seduce the analyst, he stages the same drama that is present in the dream: he wishes to become the pilot who takes over the aircraft that is the treatment; he knows how to pilot and wants to show the analyst. At first, he feels fascinating and important, but quickly, when confronted with some unsettling element, such as the end of a session, a real interpretation, or an interruption evoking the analyst's privacy or third parties in her life, he crashes and fails just as in the dream.

José has recently been going to a fertility clinic because he is planning to have children with his partner, but they have not managed to get pregnant. They thought about the option of an *in vitro* fertilisation, but the female gynaecologist who treated them tells him that he does not have good sperm for an *in vitro* fertilisation. Now they are thinking about the possibility of a donor, he is upset about the option, but feels guilty about failing his wife.

The following fragment of a session occurs a couple of days after he finds out that *in vitro* fertilisation will not work. José arrives at the session, lies down on the couch, stretches, yawns, speaks slowly, with pauses, constantly falling silent.

I've been eating vegetables and fruits for two or three days, I stopped eating junk food which I really like, now I have gastritis and colitis, it seems that it doesn't do me any good to eat healthy. These weeks have been very stressful... when I feel good at home I don't at work, and vice versa, I think I feel bad constantly... I have to find a way to eat healthy, but without my stomach resenting it... especially tangerine and carrot give me gastritis. I contacted the doctor on Tuesday night and she prescribed me an anti-inflammatory and I feel better, it helps me, it takes away the pain... I was remembering a guy who died in front of me, I was in my classroom at school, I talked about it with R who now works with me because I recommended him, he was a very good friend of the guy who died, I only knew him as an acquaintance. I wanted to know how it had affected him because it had impacted me a lot, the topic came up, but we didn't talk about it much... I'm starting to realize that I'm halfway through my life, it would be very optimistic to think that I'm going to reach eighty and I begin to realize everything I put off: a healthier diet, exercise. I think there's time, but it's not true, there's no time anymore and there never was, it's a really absurd illusion: to tell myself I'll do it later, there's i time, yet it's not true... I've been feeling a little sad; today I took Laura to work and I noticed she seemed sad, tired, in low spirits, and I think I feel that way too...

Several elements about José can be observed in this fragment: his depression and discouragement; a confusion between what helps or hurts evident in the allusion to good or bad food as well as in his reference to a doctor who previously delivers bad news and another who cures his stomach pain; his pessimism in feeling there is no time, in the memory of a young man's death, and his saying that at 33 he is halfway through his life; the strong need for a bond that sustains him, manifested in the recognition that what the doctor gave him was good and is what he needs, as well as in the feeling that he did not talk enough to R about the death of the young man. José, among other things, seems to allude to a request for food, medicine, and dialogue. It also seems that the projective distance he built in the previous dream—the one where the defeated people getting off the plane were other pilots, while José was observing in the distance—was diluted. Now the distance no longer exists, and he feels sadness and pain.

Besides what José recounts, he also produces a specific emotional climate, an atmosphere full of heaviness, slowness, and a lack of vitality. One of the technical challenges is trying to *capture* what José conveys in his speech and in his style of communication. José can be shown for instance that he feels like a paralysed sperm, unable to fertilise, slow and useless. One can point out to him that death or premature old age appear as expressions of that sterility that haunts him and seems to trap his identity, as if no vital force remained. It would also seem that the diagnosis delivered by the female doctor was experienced as a verdict that dealt him a mortal wound, like the one his schoolmate suffered, leaving him sick and old.

The hypothesis that José is identifying with the crippled, infertile sperm is a metaphorical construction, a novel way of trying to describe his depressive state. His depression is not new, José customarily places himself in imaginary loci of castration and deterioration that leave him despondent, what is original is an approach that can enrich the means available for self-observation and to give meaning to his experience. The news of his infertility seems to confirm his most pessimistic view of himself, and jolting him into awareness about this identification is fundamental for his evolution.

One advantage of metaphor is the signifying breadth and openness it brings. To speak of José's present identification with sterile, inert sperm opens up the possibility of exploring his feeling of impotence and castration, of inferiority and comparison, the very dilemma of his sterility, his attitude in the session, among other things.

Of course, in this particular session, it is advisable to emphasise José's need to feel contained and nourished in the therapeutic bond, and the doubts he manifests regarding the analyst's ability to achieve this task. One can show him that his impulse to talk more with R about the shock of his schoolmate's death has to do with his desire for the analyst to listen and attend to what disturbs him. It is also worthwhile to point out to him that when he says he requires healthy food, there is a reference to emotional and not only organic nutrition. Will the analyst be able to give him the nourishment he needs? Will this mental food contain the necessary vitamins to mobilise the sperm (himself) and achieve fertility and vitality? Will the analyst have a medicine to calm his pain? Will the analyst be like the doctor who thinks he is infertile, like a mother who does not put him in the privileged and important place of the pilot?

Previous metaphors are interwoven in the analytic dialogue, for instance, that of the pilot furnished by the previous dream. As in any significant bond, common points of reference are built; a kind of metaphorical, intimate, living, and dynamic dictionary is built during the analysis, one to which patient and analyst allude. Gradually, the conversation moves away from literalness and is strengthened in a universe of meanings and images charged with signified and re-signified emotions.

Dreams and transference[1]

Meltzer found it striking that in psychoanalytic publications dreams do not usually have the relevance one would expect. He talked about the emotional impact involved for the analyst in receiving a dream. The plastic and aesthetic force of the dream penetrates and generates countertransference reactions maybe like no other material. The impact of the dream image invades the mind. Confusion, invasion, impotence, the feeling of an excessive burden, or a fear of ignorance are some of the common emotional responses that can arise in reaction to the retelling of a dream. Like Bion, Meltzer thinks that an absence of dreams in treatments often denotes the analyst's fear to get involved, to go deeper into the intimacy implied in the communication of dreams.

In contemporary Kleinian psychoanalysis, it is considered that resistance does not arise in the face of an *insight*, but in the face of the possibility of being deeply involved in the transference. In this sense, Bion understood that patients know how to evoke in the analyst their own difficulty towards entering fully into the relationship, sensing the fear that the analyst may have towards the intensity that the bond implies. When a patient manages to participate freely in the spontaneous and fluid communication of dreams, it is because he knows the courage of the analyst and his determination to accompany him in the exploration of his mind.

Dreams developed in the analytical process are highly influenced by transference. A statement in Meltzer's *The Apprehension of Beauty—She argued, she sulked, she flattered, she wept, but fortunately she also dreamt...* (Meltzer and Harris, 1988: 139)—alludes to the power that a dream acquires when it embodies the drama of transference and often of countertransference as it unfolds in treatment.

The following dream appears during a complicated period in the treatment of a 50-year-old woman, a patient who had been undergoing analysis with me for three years, presenting serious melancholic episodes, depersonalisation, acute confusional anxieties, and a premature and persistent eroticised transference. As a child, she showed a strong possessive impulse towards her mother: she watched her mother daily from a balcony of her apartment when she left for work. Losing sight of her mother when she turned the corner, she would estimate the time it would take her to get to the office and call her on the phone. If her mother did not answer in the expected time, she would become overwhelmed with anxiety to the point of getting sick. In the analytical relationship many of these traits were repeated.

The period of analytical work during which the dream arose was characterised by constant recriminations, with a permanent feeling of anger towards me and towards the limited or inadequate nature of what I offered her given her intense sense of need. Some of her statements illustrate this emotional climate: *I must submit; speaking is my only right, my only possibility. I can't have any other relationship with you than to be here for a few miserable minutes.* Or again: *You push me away with what you say to me, you distance me, you start to push me away. I am very sorry to disappoint you; when I get like this you must feel very frustrated, poor thing, after so much progress, but you see: there are things that cannot be changed, not now or ever, so don't even say anything.*

During our sessions I described for her the constant feeling of disappointment she felt because I was not everything she expected; how painful the separation between sessions was for her, and how she experienced it as a rupture; I talked to her about the anger she felt about the asymmetry in our relationship: how she needed me and felt that she loved me while I placed myself in such a different role; also about the jealousy brought about by my absence. I tried to describe how the pain in the relationship worsened and how a situation of abuse and control was produced. However, every interpretation, every word, and even every movement seemed to be provocations on my part with the purpose of attacking or hurting her. My countertransference was one of paralysis and anger: session after session there was an unchanging feeling of remaining stuck in discomfort and irritation.

Then, a dream came:

There was a fishbowl-like tunnel. It was a machine that women came out of. You could look at it like it was a fishbowl. Then a woman came out from the tunnel, as if a stretcher glided out of the tunnel and there she was, lying down, naked, as if sleeping. She wasn't moving, at first, I thought she was dead but no. I was pulling her, kind of taking her by the arms. She was beautiful like that, still. I said I wanted a fishbowl like that, not just the woman but the fishbowl too, I wanted that fishbowl so I could take out a woman like her whenever I wanted. She was like a test-tube woman. As if you could get her from a machine.

I was greatly affected by the dream, as well as by the counter-transferential relief it brought. The painful emotional experience I had suffered in recent weeks turned into a plastic metaphor that allowed me to understand a great deal about my experience: the essential condition that made the test-tube woman perfect was her immobility. The incomprehensible paralysis I suffered in the countertransference for weeks seemed to have been captured in that scene about a woman who, to preserve her worth, had to remain inert. It seemed that the patient wanted to cling to me, to adhere by hugging, but when I spoke, moved, or manifested some kind of autonomy, it broke this illusion of fusion and possession.

There are many significant elements in the dream, various lines were opened as possible paths for exploration: the machine that creates women as an allusion to procreation but from the viewpoint of omnipotent and mechanical control of this function; beauty turned into an inert, concrete sensuality that allows one to possess the object; an envious desire to usurp the capacity of conception, the creative potential of the mother and the parental couple; the force of an intrusive curiosity towards fertilisation in the idea of being able to look through the glass, among others. However, the reason the dream was so useful for a time was that it managed to capture a nuance of our relationship and the atmosphere that was unfolding.

Weeks after the dream I was struck by something that was in fact not new, a common and constant feature in her: the hypomaniacal way she had of talking and sometimes moving, her intense and unstoppable rhythm. We had previously talked about her verboseness as a way to entrap, as if words were tentacles to capture the other, in this case, myself. That interpretation made sense to her, and she remembered how she would sit on her mother's lap and talk to her like that, taking her chin and turning her face so that she looked at her. She also remembered how her mother once fainted while she was sitting on her lap talking endlessly.

After the dream, I thought about the contrast between the inert immobility of the test-tube woman and the hyperkinesia and verbiage that she manifested. We then talked about this agitation as a way to stay alive, to distance herself from the deathlike position of the woman in the dream. She then remembered that when she was about ten years old, she saw a picture of her as a baby where her hands and feet were bandaged. She asked her mother why and her mother explained that she rubbed her feet so hard that she would get blisters and sores, and pressed her fingers so hard against the palms of her hands that it made them bleed, so she had to be bandaged as a way to prevent her from harming herself.

It would seem that the impetuous motions of the baby were both a way to somatically expel anxiety and also perhaps an attempt to not be rendered inert. By her agitation, she seemed to want to stay alive and perhaps also to vitalise the object, that is, the mother, who appears as the cold and impersonal test-tube woman.

The perspective afforded by the dream shed light on yet another angle of the transference: the need to be taken into someone's arms, to receive warmth and support, and the sense that if this does not happen, she feels treated coldly, and becomes anxious and enraged out of desperation that the object did not react.

Epilogue

Dreams are a *gold mine* for symbolic construction. If the patient cannot remember her dreams, she will be unable to express her emotions to the analyst, and the means of communication will then be to act outside or inside the transference.

> [...] With the help of dreams, which come to the rescue of this incapacity for symbol formation, his dream language begins to fashion a poetry of its own that is special to that patient and that analyst in their particular and unique transference and countertransference relationship
>
> (Meltzer, 1997: 176).

Furthermore, dreams aid the analyst by providing symbolic richness. Analysts attempt to understand patients by developing a language that generate meaning, but reaching that poetic capability is not easy. Dreams are tools that enrich the communication with the patient (Harris, 2010a).

In short, Bion and Meltzer start from the idea that life itself is devoid of meaning and it is the mind, in an act of emotional metabolism or digestion, that imparts meaning on lived experience. This process of emotional metabolism or digestion is what Bion considers thinking. Human relationships, the world, one's identity, the events of a life, the relationship with the present, the past, or the future... nothing has an intrinsic meaning, it is rather built, constructed from within mental life and at the heart of this construction of meaning is the dream.

One of Freud's great contributions was to show that dreams have meaning, and to develop a research method to study dreams and understand how they are constructed. However, Freud anchored his work on dreams in neurophysiology and quantitative conceptions. For him, dream symbols were understood as a substitution or translation without alteration or increase in meaning. In other words, the dream work did not imply constructing a meaning, which is rather given in advance. It does not imply producing something original; for Freud, dream thoughts have an existence prior to dreaming and dreams would not provide anything new. Additionally, in Freudian theory, dreams implied a regression to more primitive forms of psychic functioning[2], while for Bion and Meltzer dreams constitute the greatest creative power of the mind.

Bion thinks that emotional experience initially presents itself in disjointed form, incapable of being grasped: *raw*. A mysterious mental movement, highly artistic and symbolic, captures and apprehends these elements that then take on another status within the mind. Dreams are the core of this process, the very centre of the articulation of meaning. To stand before a dream is to witness a living, dynamic process, not only expressive but constructive of meaning, a process by which meaning is imprinted on experience.

Language is a rich tool for the description of common objects and the concrete world: size, weight, high, low, how much something costs... but it is poor for describing the emotional world. In dreams, the patient and the analyst are rescued from this linguistic poverty. Thanks to the plastic metaphor that is the dream, the poet-painter part of the patient provides a construct that captures what escapes language.

These considerations, however, should not confuse the reader regarding the problem of the mind's capacity to lie. Although dreams are *the theatre that generates meaning*, and produced by means of the richest creative resources, they might also be at the service of lies. For example, in the dream of the test-tube woman, it would seem that a tyrannical aspect of the patient's character takes over the mind. In José's case, it would seem that the initial scriptwriter of the dream is an aggrandised childish part. It is possible to construct meaning from a pathological area of the personality that reinforces the subjacent conflict.

We have said that the resources employed by the dream are artistic, both lyrical and iconographic. Poetry and the plastic faculties of the dream condense and furnish formal representation to emotional experiences. Contrary to what is sometimes assumed, when we work with dreams in analytic sessions, the understanding one gains of them implies a symbolic transformation in which the meaning and its expression are necessarily impoverished. It is an exercise similar to translating poetry into prose or trying to explain a painting.

Technical work with dreams shifts from being a *decipherment* (interpretation) to be a *description* for the purposes of *exploration*. The Meltzerian idea of *exploring* dreams rather than *analyzing* them entails a particular epistemological, aesthetic, and technical position. The differentiation between latent and manifest content is blurred. Also, it is assumed that the richness of the dream will be simplified when we resort to words. Considering dreams from this perspective invites us to assume a position of modesty, of reserve in the face of an exercise that involves a certain desecration. Interpretations will always fall short of the meanings interwoven in the dream.

The study of dreams from this perspective encourages the deployment of intervention strategies where vivid images try to capture emotionality.

In psychoanalytic technique, it is important to approach the metaphorical mechanisms of the dream in order to try to give symbolic form to emotional experience.

Of course, the level of metaphorical complexity of an interpretation depends on the patient's ability to understand; the lower the level of abstraction of the child or adult in treatment, the simpler and more basic the metaphorical approaches must be. In the case of mental structures governed by literal-mindedness, it is necessary to emphasise comparative links of the kind employed in similes.

If the analyst considers dreams as a model of thought, she will try in her clinical work to access the most creative ways in which the mind operates, offering interpretations that use simple metaphors to point out aspects of the *self*, internal objects, mechanisms of mental functioning, or emotional states. The analyst will understand that repetitive, clichéd, and routine interventions should be avoided, and prefer colloquial, simple, and descriptive interventions that have a stronger emotional effect, being more vivid and authentic.

The psychoanalytic method is a vital descriptive exercise in which the patient finds a story, an image, or a metaphor that leads to a recognition and a more subtle understanding of the self, enabling the discovery of previously unknown aspects of its inner life.

Notes

1 Excerpt taken from Ortiz, E. *Donald Meltzer. Vida onírica. Sueños, mente y pensamiento,* 2019: 130–134.
2 Topographic regression. In the dream state thoughts are denied their access to motility and return to the perceptual pole. The excitation takes a reverse direction where thoughts are presented in the form of sensory images (Freud, 1900).

Bibliography

APdeBA (1999), "Laura", in *Diálogos clínicos con Donald Meltzer,* Buenos Aires, APdeBA, pp. 179–195.

Bion, Wilfred (1962), "The Psychoanalytic Study of Thinking", *International Journal of Psycho-Analysis,* 43: 306–310. Also in *Second Thoughts,* London, Heinman.

Calich, José Carlos (2022), Introducción a la mesa "Darío". La conversación más interesante del mundo, APdeBA, Homenaje a Donald Meltzer a 100 años de su nacimiento, Inédito.

Del Palacio, Jaime (2019), "Prólogo del editor" in Ortiz, Elena, *Donald Meltzer. Vida onírica. Sueños, mente y pensamiento,* México, Analytiké.

Freud, Sigmund (1900), *La interpretación de los sueños,* Buenos Aires, Amorrortu Editores, 1989. Also, in *The Interpretation of Dreams,* New York, Basic Books.

Harris W., Meg (1983), "'Underlying Pattern' in Bion's *Memoir of the Future*", *International Review of Psycho-Analysis,* 10: 75–86.

—— (2010a), *The Aesthetic Development. The Poetic Spirit of Psychoanalysis. Essays on Bion, Meltzer, Keats*, London, Karnac.

—— (ed.) (2010b), *A Meltzer Reader. Selections from the Writings of Donald Meltzer*, London, Karnac.

Meltzer, Donald (1984), *Dream Life: A Re-examination of the Psycho-analytical Theory and Technique*, Perthshire, Clunie Press.

—— (1995), "On the Cruelty of Symbol Formation", in Meg Harris W. (Ed.), *A Meltzer Reader. Selections from the Writings of Donald Meltzer*, pp. 122–123, London, Karnac, 2010.

—— (1997), "Concerning Signs and Symbols", in *British Journal of Psychotherapy*, 14(2): 175–181.

Meltzer, Donald and Meg Harris W. (1988), *The Apprehension of Beauty. The Role of Aesthetic Conflict in Development, Art and Violence*, London, Karnac.

Meltzer, Donald, Mariella Albergame, Eve Cohen, Alba Greco, Martha Harris, Susanna Maiello, Giuliana Milana, Diomira Petrelli, Maria Rhode, Anna Sabatini Scolmati, Francesco Scotti (1986), *Studies in Extended Metapsychology: Clinical Applications of Bion's Ideas*, London, The Roland Harris Educational Trust Library.

Ortiz, Elena (2019), *Donald Meltzer. Vida onírica. Sueños, mente y pensamiento*, México, Analytiké.

—— (2023), *Donald Meltzer, Actualizaciones en psicoanálisis. Un estudio sobre su obra*, México, Eleia.

Sharpe, Ella (1937), *Dream Analysis*, London, Karnac, 1988.

8 Introjection, intimacy and object relations

Carlos Tabbia (2023)

Meltzer (1978, p. 458) considered introjection to be "the most important and most mysterious concept in psychoanalysis". This is by no means an excessive statement, considering that the development of internal objects and psychic reality depends on introjection. The capacity for intimacy is, in turn, dependent on the quality of the introjections. Both depend on the quality of the relationship with external and internal objects.

One of the mysterious aspects of introjection—the basis of growth and development—is the paradoxical rejection of the incorporation of objects. For this reason, after discriminating the limits of the term introjection, I will present a series of clinical vignettes showing that the difficulty in relating with the object hinders introjection and, consequently, the possibility of intimacy.

The correlation between oral impulses and introjection (Ferenczi, 1909) was one of the first steps in the discovery of the mysterious—also for Freud, according to Hinshelwood (1989)—phenomenon of introjection. Without a doubt, the collaboration with Abraham was essential to unravel that a phenomenon capable of provoking transformations[1] in the personality as a consequence of the incorporation of objects that existed previously in the external world. When referring to the incorporation of objects from the external world into the internal world, we are reminded of the famous dispute about the equivalence between introjection and incorporation. Whereas some authors differentiate between them, others use them as synonyms; for example, Laplanche & Pontalis (1968) state that Freud and many other authors use them synonymously. This is the case, for example, of Betty Joseph (2015). Even though the corporal model of introjection is the oral mode, this does not mean that referring to the phantasy of incorporation implies a concrete action. Beyond the cannibalistic action characteristic of all incorporation, no human action is without a meaning: that of introducing something into one's personal perimeter. When Bion was reflecting on drive theory, he borrowed the term "tropism" from biology but later dropped that term. It is precisely from its biological basis that this term implies the search for objects (light, oxygen, moisture, etc.) as a condition for the viability of life. P. Sandler (2005, pp. 805/806) says that by

DOI: 10.4324/9781003441861-9

using this term, "Bion was trying to investigate the mysterious nature of movements towards life itself and their obverse". However, the relationship with objects does not always strive towards life, but, as Bion himself proposed, there are those who seek "murder, parasitism and creativity" (Bion, 1991). On many occasions, patients, including adults, verbalise the desire to eat the analyst as a primitive manifestation of the longing to introject them. Such was the case of a patient, a Spanish artist, as intelligent as he was borderline psychotic, who told me that I looked like a Patagonian, a tall, strong, powerful inhabitant of Argentinian Patagonia. Later, after the session had finished, he referred to the Spanish conquistadors who, in the era of discovery in the sixteenth century, while starving, anchored in a bay, seduced a Patagonian man with trinkets, captured him and eventually ate him. I hope, humourously, that in this patient's tropisms, it is creativity that predominates over the other two.[2]

Continuing with a model capable of elucidating the mysteries of the mind and psychoanalysis, such as introjection, I find Wisdom's (1961, 1963) scheme for representing mental organisation to be suggestive and even didactic. In his diagram, his conceptualisation, he differentiates between the outer world and the self, and, within the self, the orbital zone (the first territory for the introjected objects) and the nucleus of the self (the repository of the refined introjective identifications). The first differentiation of "outer world/object" and "self" is of particular significance because it is the first step in the construction of the personality and overcoming possible psychotic confusion. When an object from external reality is allowed to enter into internal reality, it is permitted to move freely within the internal orbit. Here is where the intra-psychic relationship between objects begins; in that territory, the distillation of experiences and a future assumption of functions and qualities become possible. They progressively become part of the identity, concentrated in the nucleus of the self through introjective identifications. I agree with Grinberg (1976, p. 36) when he states that "the internalisation of an object involves granting it space inside the mental apparatus. In unconscious phantasy, the object is experienced as coming and going freely, doing as it wishes". This is precisely what is not observed in patients with very primitive anxieties, as I will present below. In each vignette, a particular feature can be observed regarding the introjection phantasy. Amongst these peculiarities, I will point out the opposition against an object moving freely within the orbit.

This theme manifests itself in the case of **Inés** (Meltzer et al., 2003), a tiny restless 11-month-old baby who had great difficulty eating or feeding from the breast or a bottle. This difficulty, along with the fear that she might die, motivated her parents to request the consultation. During the hour of observation, first with the mother, then with the father, it could be seen that every one of Inés' initiatives was interfered with by her parents. This interference generated a sensation that Inés was controlled and subjected to the paternal desires to stimulate or even save her.

The paradox in this situation was that, to a certain degree, the anxious parental clash provoked the opposite effect. In this case, the child can choose to withdraw from the scene and dismantle contact with the object. An added problem with Inés' defensive action was her denial to grant a place in her interior for the maternal offers, which ended up exhausting her mother. Given this sterile cycle, Meltzer et al. (2003, p. 209) stated,

> this is how autistic children are made, how they are formed. It is one of the ways in which autistic children appear overwhelmed and crushed, by the parents' hijacking any sort of initiative that may appear, and the parents may even laugh at the child, humiliate them, or treat them like clowns. They gradually let themselves fall, sliding towards autistic inaccessibility.

This slide towards inaccessibility not only allows Inés to avoid anything entering her inner world but also denies her any kind of intimacy. Similar experiences to that of Inés can happen during the analytic session, when the analyst does not respect the analysand's timing and ways of relating and overwhelms them. With Inés, we observe that *difficulties in introjecting* can sometimes arise from a certain parental inability to observe and grasp meaning in child behaviour, together with the infant's defensive immaturity.[3]

Nevertheless, **Inés** is a child that learns, is feminine, delicate, and temperamental but avoids being invaded; she has been able to introject enough experiences to differentiate invasive relationships from others. This is not so in the case of **David**, a demanding, tyrannical, jealous five-year-old, who constantly challenges everything, e.g. he refuses to eat and even spits out his food... David is a child who experienced foetal suffering during birth and possibly minimal brain damage. Given the child's overall situation, Meltzer et al. (2002, p. 137) stated that:

> ...his introjective capacity is limited, and in his internal world he has not yet been able clearly to distinguish between the presence and absence of the object. [...] As for the diagnosis, he would be described as a hyperactive child who is gradually getting better. His capacity for symbol formation is still fragile, and his sense of identity is easily swallowed up by the various kinds of narcissistic identifications. [...] There are still rather serious problems of confusion. To sum up, we can find immaturity, problems with confusion, with introjection, and, basically, primitive catastrophic anxieties.

In David's material, we can see that this *difficulty to introject, his limited capacity*, resides in the fact that he has not yet been able to clearly differentiate between the presence and absence of the object.

Montse's state of mind was different from David's. She was an attractive woman in her thirties, married without children, diagnosed with schizophrenia, and was still far from being prepared to tolerate introjection. Amongst other motives, this was because, as Meltzer (op. cit., p. 158) diagnosed,

> ...she is totally out of contact with her psychic reality, with her fantasies, with her feelings. It is not only a matter of being out of contact with all this but also that she is determined to stay out of contact with all this. We find ourselves seeing a personality who is extremely strongly determined to persist in this project.

For her, satisfaction did not stem from the fact that something could enter her inner world, her orbit, but—as Meltzer, op. cit, p. 169/170 said—that something could leave

> ...something very good is experienced as being clean, as evacuating everything that is troubling; but it is very difficult for them to introject. They are very deficient introjectors. [...] She is a very deficient introjector, and she cannot make herself responsible for what she has introjected. When she has emptied herself through masturbation, she feels confused and she has confused and riling thoughts.

Her strong, self-sufficient character was based upon denying her inner world and was affirmed by a determined *opposition to any kind of introjection.* Her great ability to project complemented this attitude. While believing herself to be the saviour of the world and the ambassador of universal peace, she projected her anxiety onto her environment, thus managing to make many people worried about her. In view of this, Meltzer (ibid, p. 159) stated that:

> one can't take everything she says as the truth and nothing but the truth, because she is not an honest communicator, she is an inveterate projector. The question to ask oneself is whether all of what she refers to are hallucinations or masturbatory phantasies. My opinion is that it is the latter – masturbatory phantasies.

Masturbatory phantasies derived from intrusive identifications that generated a triumphant sensation of superiority, with which she could dazzle or fascinate.

In contrast to those who cannot introject, such as Inés or David, or those who refuse to, such as Montse, there are those who are capable of doing so but avoid the experience due to envy, omnipotence, or obstructiveness. They usually introject but do so covertly, resorting to enforced splitting (Bion, 1962); in this way, they obtain what they need for survival, but without having to recognise it Operating this way, however, does not provide a satisfying experience, and growth and development are seriously hindered. This was the situation of **Graciela**, a 12-year-old girl with anorexia, who refused to eat, defiantly interrogating and troubling close family members with questions such as "Why do we need to eat? Why do we have to live?". In the supervision of this material, Meltzer (1999, p. 122) showed how the patient was "very worried about projecting depressive anxieties onto everyone", especially her parents, with very typical behaviour of an anorexic patient. While these patients project, they avoid introjecting, instead using arrogant argumentation, with typical "obsessive rumination, to avoid having emotional experiences. To leave it all in the conscious, they block being receptive to what people think, or to having an emotional experience with another person". Their omnipotence makes them sacrifice all introjection and its derived emotionality, thereby destroying any meaning. An expression of the defiant and arrogant attitude of this anorexic functioning is expressed in a song, sung by a pubescent girl, that was popular amongst adolescents, the lyrics said, "… I'd rather be dead than plain". Graciela's resistance was heightened following a holiday, to the point where she snapped at the analyst: "You're nobody". Meltzer (1999, p. 129/130) saw this sentence as "…important evidence of omnipotence; she is a bit like a baby who can annihilate objects by the process of not looking at them…" but to do so calls for "…a first process of introjection, modification and annihilation of the external object. She introjects with her gaze, modifying the object to her convenience; in this way, she has the objects that she wants inside of herself, and then she can annihilate the external object without paying it any attention". Clearly, it is impossible to annihilate an object without first introducing it into the orbital of the self and modifying it according to her intentions. However, in Graciela, both the desire to eliminate the analyst, and favourable changes (she was gaining weight which made her feminine traits become more visible) coexisted which could be explained by the analytical bond. I think these changes resulted from the enforced splitting: while she rejected the analyst, she introjected her consciously and unconsciously, but without cknowledging it, to not re-establish ambivalence or offend her narcissism, nor to thank her. In this case, *introjection was substituted by disguised theft*.

Meltzer (ibid, p. 142) compared Graciela's behaviour to some of the manoeuvres of psychotic patients who "are capable of stealing internal objects and replacing them with their own, dilapidated objects" with the risk of inadvertently introjecting them through the object, be it the analyst or the parents. These patients may often appear very intelligent but raise enough doubts about the origin of their knowledge, whether it is based on emotional experiences or, instead, is learned through accumulation, mimicry or simple adhesion or theft. Graciela's difficulty in introjecting and introjectively identifying herself with free and autonomously recognised objects raised doubts for Meltzer (ibid, p. 143), who warned: "...There is no doubt that the manifest improvement that appears via this psychotic manoeuvre cannot succeed in producing the patient's development [...] because she is incorporating an aged, desexualised, mother; a mother that is dying and will ultimately make her ill in the form of depression and hypochondria. [...] that is to say that she can deceive the analyst and make them believe that she is getting better and that she can leave already" to finish the "treatment in a manic way". I think that Meltzer indicates that in her introjecting/stealing, Graciela has not chosen good objects, but rather spoiled ones, which locks her in hypochondriacal anorexia. Far from introjecting autonomous objects, she has opted for a false identity derived from the intrusive identification with parental objects but deprived of all mutual and reparative intimacy, similar to Hamm, the character in Beckett's (1957) *Endgame*. Just like Hamm, while she controlled the relationship between her devitalised parents, she lacked the freedom to learn, that is, to introject. To achieve an adult state of mind, one must abandon narcissistic gratification derived from the confusion of identity typical in pseudo-mature subjects or those trapped in hypochondriacal anorexia.

The arrogance seen in hypochondriacal states usually deceives us because it gives us the sensation of stability and security. Conversely, anorexia nervosa is turbulent, oscillating between voracious binge eating and self-induced vomiting. The difference between these two lies in the fact that in hypochondriacal anorexia, the subject believes itself to be the object, whereas in anorexia nervosa, the subject cannot introject it. These patients cannot feel the pain of the impossibility of introjecting without abandoning the confusion with the object (via intrusive identification). Only then can the infantile transference begin to emerge in the analytic relationship, enabling the child's mouth to see the analytic nipple for the first time in a long time, and the steps towards an intimate relationship to be taken.

Rocío's deceptions

Earlier, I mentioned deception and fascination, another form of deception. In these cases, we were dealing with states of mind derived from difficulty in establishing dependent relationships with objects. At the heart of these states lay distrust. This was Rocío's situation.

The first time I met **Rocío**, she told me that she was being treated by a psychiatrist to whom "I didn't tell everything". She thought this could be a motive for her not having received enough help despite her many years of treatment. I wondered: what was it that she could not communicate openly? What did "everything" mean? Did she know what she wanted to communicate? Was she resisting voluntarily and choosing to hide/deceive through withholding? Etc. My surprise grew as I discovered an intelligent, introspective young woman in her first years of university. I soon discovered this curious young woman coexisted with a pseudo-mature personality, trapped in a claustrophobic world.

One of the first things that aroused my curiosity was a particular scenography that was created to keep a distance from me in the interviews. Other patients with a state of mind similar to that of Rocío's are capable of trying to protect themselves from the analyst's presence, attempting to build a wall around themselves, whether with objects (their glasses, books, coats, etc., placed to form an enveloping wall behind which they seem to hide), or with torrents of verbal communication, which, like waterfalls, prevent contact with the speaker, or shielded behind long-lasting expectant silences. Rocío's hyper-vigilant attitude and the distance she created in general could be illustrated by the following situations related in the initial interviews. One was a childhood fantasy that she used to have while sitting in the back seat of the family car. From that vantage point, she would look out the window at the pedestrians and cut them in two with her eyes, like razor blades. Another material corroborating this fantasy was a dream she related at the time:

> I cut open my belly horizontally with a knife. That's how I punished someone. There were people around me. Dark men in hats. Women too. I saw the pink flesh and the red blood. I felt no pain. Then I emptied myself out completely and I ended up like a shell, with black eyeholes. I bought myself a coat and dark glasses. There was a child there. Later, I saw myself walking in a park with my aunt, wearing the coat and glasses. I thought: *they don't know how [empty] I'm feeling.*

She related this dream without emotion, and without pain. Given that it came from material from the initial interviews, it could not be elaborated; nevertheless, it was later possible to grasp some meaning from this dream material. Just as she used the razor to punish everyone who approached her territory, in the same way, she emptied herself, eliminating everything that was not herself from her world. This generated in her a triumphant feeling of eliminating the objects, of fooling everyone, and at the same time generating the illusion of independence. In this way, her eyes/razors/emptying cannot fulfil their incorporative function, but to the contrary: they project destruction. By fearing introjection, and therefore not being able to construct a psychic endoskeleton, Rocío chose a shell as her protective exoskeleton. And while she rejected the external world, she was deceitful.

The natural consequence of this rejection was a depressive but not melancholic state. I differentiate between these two based on the attitude towards the objects and, fundamentally, on their quality. In this case, Rocío's phantasy of emptying herself of objects refers to a state of mind characteristic of neurotic depression resulting from the impossibility of introjecting objects. This type of depression is distinct from the melancholic depression that arises from introjective identification with destroyed, devalued, and dead objects.

But a doubt remained over what the nature of the object was that she wanted to punish by eliminating everything that was not herself. I think we may find an answer in Rocío's emotional world, where distrust of the object's intentions, deception, disillusion, trickery, and resentment occupied a lot of space. On this occasion, a dream allowed the origins of her distrust to be observed. To understand the meanings of this dream, it is worth pointing out that the patient had great ambivalence towards the penis; not only the father but also the analyst himself was observed with suspicion. She could not discriminate if the penis was an alternative to the frustrating nipple or a sadistic object that will first seduce her and then frustrate her. This phantasy was nothing more than a partial and ill-fated consequence of her longing to invite the penis into her interior and thereby control it. Her yearning to control the penis not only formed part of the oedipal rivalry, but also of her intention to prevent the analyst from having all the information possible because, in this case, she thought she would be controlled. This reminds me of a claustrophobic girl who, while in the family car, always stuck her finger out of the window to avoid the anxiety of being at the mercy of the object. Whereas at the start, Rocío had stated that she did not tell her psychiatrist everything, at this point in the analysis, she had made progress towards a more sincere communication with the psychiatrist and with me; surely, my intervention—in which I acknowledged her growing trust in both—could have been felt by her to be complacent and/or seductive. I believe that this intervention prompted the following dream. It was a single scene where

> there was a group of people. We had to go through various tests. We had to take our clothes off. We were naked and were not ashamed. One of the tests was a trail leading to a place in the centre of the earth—hell. We walked down stone steps, an increasingly narrow tube, like an inverted cone. We descended, and in the corner, there was a kind of trap, and we couldn't get out. It was a deadly trap; we would die there. There was excrement in that space, —the patient said she had had more than one dream with excrement all over the place and that she had not told me, and she picked up the narrative of the dream again— we couldn't get out; it was a kind of trick.

In the supervision of this material, when Meltzer reached thought of this dream of condensed symbolisation, he considered that deception seemed to be at the centre of the dream. The deception is realised through the undressing that leads to an impasse. In this case, he would have interpreted this material as a dream about her fingers going into her anus (cf. anal masturbation with subsequent intrusion and entrapment in the

Claustrum). When her fingers enter her rectum, this initially produces an exhilarating sensation, but once the fingers touch faeces, she realises it is a deception, a trap, forever. I think that this dream and its meaning derive from my intervention; Rocío had transformed it into an invitation from the therapeutic partner—as a parental partner—to enter into our sexual relationship; that is to say, into our intimacy. However, far from finding pleasure and well-being, she found herself, to the contrary, tricked and trapped in the faeces; furthermore, trapped with the added threat of being expelled into the sewer—madness—in a clear edition of the phantasies of the inhabitants of the rectal compartment. There were many occasions in which Rocío was worried she was crazy, or distrusted the object's intentions, for example, fearing she would be seduced and then abandoned.

Apart from the difficulty of differentiating objects' intentions, there is the added difficulty that these pseudo-mature people have in getting close to other people. It is the above-mentioned issue of distance. Rocío could not regulate the distance from the object, nor the opening of her mouth/mind. This reminds me that Meltzer had sometimes illustrated the difficulty some animals have in approaching people to take something being offered to them, as if, when shown an appetising treat, they cannot judge the distance and, faced with this, may either lunge at the hand and bite the fingers, or quickly retreat into their house/cave and isolate themselves. Rocío's fear of traps prompted her to insistently assess my willingness to treat her, and to be vigilant of those who came near her space/home/cave. Nevertheless, although her claustrophobic anxieties gradually subsided, her difficulties in introjecting me as a transference object and as a person still manifested themselves. It was not without pain that she expressed that she feared me.

I think that while her trend towards deceitfulness gave her a sensation of triumph, it also prevented a genuine bond with the first object and with me in the transference. However, due to the fear of an intimate relationship, it was easier for her to relate to generalisations, such as institutions or roles, than to people, and so she could treat me as impersonally as telling me that I was an analyst. She was a long way from perceiving me as a person.

The inhabitants of the *Claustrum* (Meltzer, 1992), like most borderline psychotics, are so afraid of incorporating someone in their world, that—technically—it requires great tact on the part of the psychoanalyst to let them take the initiative. Only when they invite can they open their mouth/ears/mind. To do so, they must dodge the obstacles arising from zonal confusion. (Is it a nipple or a penis being offered? Are they putting their fingers in their vagina or their anus—cf. the tunnel dream?) Amid so much uncertainty, Rocío was trying to open up so that something could get out and something could get in, that is, explore and allow projection and introjection. For this experience, the incipient trust she was experiencing in her relationship with her analyst was fundamental.

After finishing this tour through clinical material, we can point out some of the conditions necessary to make the emotional experience of introjection possible. **Inés'** case illustrates the difficulties that arise if one does not have a container-object capable of collecting both the thrust of the demands that arise from its own interior, expressed through dreams, occurrences or impulses, as well as the offers of the external world.

To do this, one needs to have established a minimum discrimination between internal and external worlds—something much more difficult for **David**. **Montse** was in the opposite situation; she maintained a staunch opposition between both worlds, wide enough for her to project on a massive scale, stubbornly and paranoidly avoiding any introjections. Although **Graciela** could discriminate between both worlds, she resisted acknowledging her dependence on the object and opted for a disguised theft of the object's qualities. Rocío was experiencing something similar. She distrusted the object, and devoted herself to controlling it, fearing being deceived, and admitting that something could enter her interior. I believe I have illustrated different aspects of states of mind trapped in paranoid-schizoid organisations that were far from a depressive relationship characterised by the object's freedom. These states were characterised by the subject's difficulty with, or clear opposition to, the object's free movement, and wanted to prevent it; as Meltzer (1978, pp. 465/466) said, the

> coming and going of the mother's breast, which stays only a moment to fill the baby and must be allowed to go its way, is also the prototype of the emotional experience, which satisfies only insofar as the object can be allowed its freedom.

Whereas the object's autonomy aroused distrust, its control provokes entrapment, claustrophobia, and despair, anaesthetised by a dose of triumph. But the challenge that remains is, that, without filling the lamp with oil, it will no longer give off light. There is no symbolic development without introjection.

When I wrote "The Concept of Intimacy in Meltzer's Thought" (2023 [2010]), I highlighted that one of the founding elements of the experience of intimacy was the acknowledgement of the "distance" between subject and object, something that David has not yet sufficiently achieved. The other foundation was the possibility of "'trusting" built on the tolerance of the autonomous coming and going of the object. These foundations were almost non-existent in the cases presented. Without these requisites, it would be impossible to open oneself up to the encounter with the other, and to experience the projective-introjective interplay. For this reason, in another paper (Tabbia, 2010, p. 118), I stated that we consider to be "intimate" that:

private space where the participants exchange affections—both loving and hostile—without being able to anticipate an outcome. This will depend on the drive interplay, the state of the internal objects of the participants of the encounter, and the interplay of introjective and projective identification. Intimacy in the adult state of mind is an experience in which the same experience modifies both participants; in this sense, one can recover the Bionian concept of *at-one-ment*, oneness, which describes the possibility of participating in the experience of forming something unprecedented, intense, and unconscious with the other which generates nostalgia and sustains itself in solitude and tolerance of the endless mystery of the other.

I have not made enough reference in this text to the fact that this experience modifies the quality of internal objects. It should be mentioned that it is an introjected object/breast that, in psychic reality, can transform psychic objects. Meltzer (1967, p. 88) asserted this when he said that:

> while the introjective activity at the breast (Chapter IV) in the analytic process, through its archaic significance, produces the quality of the objects, it is the interpretive process, I suggest, that alters the equipment of the internal objects and thus, through introjective identification, gradually of the adult part of the self.

However, based on his experience, Meltzer (1986) went on to clarify that the interpretative process did not lie in the accuracy of the interpretation, nor in the urgency to interpret, nor in an explanatory function, nor in being the sole responsibility of the analyst, but in the function of the dyadic Work group. This group must be capable of creating a container constituted by "the reciprocal adequacy of the analyst's attention and bonding and the patient's collaborative tendency, which form and seal the container, furnishing it with the degree of flexibility and robustness needed at any given moment". Therefore, I believe that having this container/dyadic Work group[4] is essential in order to produce "an 'emotional experience' that can be utilized for thinking" and that becomes "...the essential precondition for introjection" (Meltzer, 1978, p. 466).

Notes

1 As Abraham's hair bleached after the death of his of his graying father.
2 Bion (1991, p. 35) says: "...taken as a whole, and not individually, the action appropriate to the tropisms in the patient who comes for treatment is a seeking for an object with which projective identification is possible. This is due to the fact that in such a patient the tropism of creation is stronger than the tropism of murder". A noteworthy fact about this exotic and spectacularly creative patient is that he came seeking treatment because he feared his violent outbursts might have led him to kill a work colleague.

3   In this case, Inés was not finding a container-object capable of receiving communicative projective identifications On this matter, Bion (1991, p. 34) said that sometimes the tropisms of both the parents and the baby "are too powerful for the modes of communication available to the personality [...] This, presumably, may be because the personality is too weak or ill-developed if the traumatic situation arrives prematurely [...] But when this situation does arise, all the future development of the personality depends on whether an object, the breast, exists into which the tropisms can be projected. If it does not, the result is disaster which ultimately takes the form of loss of contact with reality, apathy, or mania...". This idea is present in Meltzer's later comment in relation to Inés' withdrawal from the experience.

4   Although initially the greatest responsibility falls on the object.

References

Beckett, S. (1957): *Fin de Partie*, París: Les Éditions de minuit.

Bion, W. R. (1962): *Learning from Experience*, London: Karnac.

Bion, W. R. (1991): *Cogitations*. F. Bion (ed.). London: Karnac.

Grinberg, L. (1976): *Teoría de la identificación*, Buenos Aires: Paidós.

Ferenczi (1909): Introjektion und Übertragung, *First Contr., Jb.*

Hinshelwood, R. D. (1989): *A Dictionary of Kleinian Thought*, London: Free Association Books.

Joseph, B. (2015): "La transferencia", en Bronstein, C. (ed.): *La Teoría Kleiniana. Una perspectiva contemporánea*, Madrid: Biblioteca Nueva.

Laplance, J. & Pontalis, J. P., (1968): *Vocabulaire de la Psychanalyse*, Paris: PUF.

Meltzer, D. (1967): *The Psycho-analytical Process*, Perthshire, Scotland: Clunie Press, 1990.

Meltzer, D. (1978): "A note on introjective process", in A. Hahn (ed.): *Sincerity and other Works. Collected Papers of Donald Meltzer*, London: Karnac, 1994, 458–468.

Meltzer, D. (1986): "Riflessioni sui mutamenti nel mio metodo psicoanalitico", en Morag Harris Maio e Noemi Pastino (eds.): *Psicoterapia e Scienze Umane*, Milán, 1986, XX, 3: 260–269.

Meltzer, D. (1992): *The Claustrum. An Investigation of Claustrophobic Phenomena*, Great Britain: The Clunie Press.

Meltzer, D. (1999): Diálogos clínicos con Donald Meltzer, *Psicoanálisis APdeBA* – Vol. XXI – N° 1/2, 119–145.

Meltzer, D, & Psychoanalytic Group of Barcelona & C. M. Smith (2002): *Psychoanalytic Work with Children and Adults. Meltzer in Barcelona*, London: Karnac.

Meltzer, D., C. McSmith, et al. (2003): *Bebés. Una experiencia desde un vértice psicoanalítico*, Barcelona: Grafein ediciones.

Sandler, P. C. (2005): *The Language of Bion. A Dictionary of Concepts*, London: Karnac.

Tabbia, C. (2010): "La intimidad", in *De la angustia y otros afectos*, Gradiva, Barcelona: Grafein editors, 109–120.

Tabbia, C. (2010): "The Concept of Intimacy in Meltzer's Thought", in *The Clinical Comprehension of Meaning. The Bion/Meltzer vertex*, London: Routledge, 2023.

Wisdom, J. O (1961): "A Methodological Approach to the Problem of Hystery", *International Journal of Psychoanalysis* 42, 224–237.

Wisdom, J. O. (1962). Comparison and development of the psychoanalytical theories of melancholia. International Journal of Psycho-Analysis, 43: 113–132.

9 The aesthetic model in psychoanalytic practice

Virginia Ungar, M.D.

"When one's teachers have gone, there is only their internalized representation to keep one within the bounds of a living tradition, but narcissism being as subtly invasive as it is, one can never be quite sure" (Meltzer 1986: 21). I have chosen this quotation from Meltzer as a starting point because it has always seemed to me to be the essence of a central aspect to the thinking of the master, who, as a teacher, is also gone. His presence is felt very strongly in the internal world of those who experience his teachings and also in psychoanalytic debates taking place nowadays, almost 20 years after his death.

I would like to explore the possible meaning of the idea of "a living tradition," delving especially into what this expression means to us in the world we are currently living in, one filled with uncertainty owing it to the pandemic, the climate change tragedy and the war in Europe, a world in which psychoanalysis is needed more than ever.

Let us begin by looking into the word "tradition." The Oxford English Dictionary provides the following definition: from Latin *traditio, -onem*, 'a delivery, a surrender, a handing-down; a saying handed down, a doctrine or instruction delivered.'

Tradition is, therefore, a 'handing-down,' a 'delivery.' Many times in his body of work, Meltzer refers to the fact that psychoanalysis can be learnt but, paradoxically, cannot be taught. It can thus be said that learning is facilitated, transmitted rather than taught. In his short (but important) article on the "atelier" system (1971), he described it as an exercise in craftsmanship to be given a place resembling the one represented in the monumental work of Raphael Sanzio, *The School of Athens*. This masterpiece depicts a space assembling relaxed-looking masters of philosophy of the like of Socrates, Plato, Aristotle and Parmenides; gods such as Apollo and Minerva; scientists such as Archimedes and other people who are depicted as listening and surely asking questions.

In a way, this is a similar experience to that of those who were lucky enough to have met Meltzer, to have attended his seminars, to have been

DOI: 10.4324/9781003441861-10

supervised by him and to have shared meals, walks and tango with him here in Buenos Aires, or flamenco in Spain.

I first encountered the works of Meltzer quite early on, soon after having started my work with patients, when I read *The Psycho-Analytical Process* (1967). It is a difficult book if ever there was one; it is cryptic, and one can only begin to understand it when one has weathered many analytic storms—which one has perhaps overcome with more failures than victories—and after having finally realized that one is irremediably tied to the practice of psychoanalysis by some sort of blind love.

As a child analyst, for example, if I did not approach my work from a passionate standpoint—in Meltzer's terms, the response to aesthetic objects in the indissoluble concurrence of L, H and K—how could I explain to myself the countless hours I spend in a room listening, speaking quietly, seated on a tiny chair or on the floor, watching children draw, talk or keep quiet for long periods of time, and often understanding very little of it all? Moreover, without this approach, how could I explain all the time I play enthusiastically with children, or my having listened to endless stories of successful or frustrated adolescent love, or to detailed reports on how the bass sounds on the chord of a song I have never heard?

The same is true with older patients. At times, everything seems to be rather quiet, and they do not appear to make progress through analytic work. In these occasions, it is worth remembering Meltzer's wisdom: much of our work is a routine; only a small part of it is inspiration.

I believe that the limits of the living tradition may easily refer to the Meltzerian understanding of the analytic setting. During clinical work, his students learnt to detach themselves from the formal way of conceptualizing the setting, they were encouraged to disregard parameters of time and space so as to situate themselves at the very heart of the psychoanalytic concept of the term setting, whose true epicentre is considered to be in the mental state of the analyst.

I think that the concept of the setting in psychoanalysis essentially very lively as one can think about it as the combination of the analyst's free-floating attention and the patient's free association. It also includes established formalities, like the duration and number of sessions, or other aspects such as the use of the couch and the chair as well as the payment of a fee, to name a few examples.

An interruption in free-floating attention, whether brought about by an outburst of emotions or a fantasy, that is, a countertransference experience, could possibly lead to an action on the part of the analyst that can cause a breakdown of the setting. In such circumstances, evident changes affecting the setting parameters are quite easy to pinpoint, while others causing an analyst to act in an obvious or subtle way are not. This produces a situation encompassed in the concept of *enactment*, which is strongly re-emerging in current literature on psychoanalysis.

The setting then constitutes the technical aspect of the analytic method, and according to Meltzer, it is the safeguard that is available to us analysts to avoid transgressing the technique. Transgression here refers to any interruption of the free-floating attention or free association that could lead to an enactment on both sides. However, it should not be turned into a refuge or shell that can suffocate analysts' creativity and stop him/her from allowing a degree of flexibility which, if implemented, could contribute to the analysis.

In Freud's definition of the analytic method, investigation and therapy come together. The latter is rooted on the model of the mind upheld by each therapist in accordance with their own theoretical references.

I get the impression that we, psychoanalysts, are sometimes unaware of the therapeutic nature of the method we use of. I believe that we must focus on and make explicit the nature of the analytic method. There is no doubt that psychoanalysis is currently under threat which is reflected on the healthcare institutions' unwillingness to prescribe analytic treatment. In my opinion, this favours the use of medication and makes evidence the contemporary demand for quick results implied in educational entities, which strive to maintain children on a track that seems to be designed for guaranteed social success.

It is important here to raise the point that another pillar of resistance to analysis is to be found in ourselves, psychoanalysts. This is what the second part of this chapter's initial quotation points to. Meltzer gifted us with yet another great teaching when saying that with "narcissism, being as subtly invasive as it is, one can never be quite sure." This notion is based on the work of Bion, who encouraged us analysts to look for the power of resistance, not only in our patients, but also in the ease with which the patients manage to release analysts' resistance.

This issue is closely linked with the concept of *analytic attitude*, a notion that is hard to define. First, it is necessary to look again at two other concepts that are dear to psychoanalysis: *analytic neutrality*—never mentioned by Freud, and still cited at length—and *the rule of abstinence*. The two may be considered interrelated, in the sense that neutrality, as an aspiration, relies on the rule of abstinence. I shall disregard the present discussion concerning the possibility of the analyst remaining "neutral" since, in reality, psychoanalysts are not able to meet the *realist hypothesis* of classical science suggesting that observation does not alter the observed actions, nor vice versa. It must certainly be admitted that the presence of an observer produces effects on the field of observation, and in turn, on the object of observation. It is on this impact caused by the object on the field and the field on the object that the crucial element of analysis is to be found: the transference-countertransference relationship. The rule of abstinence is, therefore, at the very core of the analytic attitude, though not in the sense of a prescriptive theory. I believe that when an analyst fails to fulfil the demands of a patient and rather responds from their analytic position in the analytic setting, the analyst do not do so because satisfaction should not be provided, but because he <u>cannot</u> supply what the patient hopes and asked of him.

What I believe to be essential of the analytic attitude is receptivity, availability and observation, open-mindedness in the face of mystery and the unknown, and an inclination to think before taking action.

The impact of the aesthetic model in our daily practice

These ideas led me to think about the position of the analyst and propose, following Meltzerian thinking, *a possible aesthetic model of the mind*. With this in mind, I will concentrate on what the master had studied his predecessors' models. Thus, in 2000 I presented the idea of a possible *aesthetic model* (2000), which stems from Meltzer's ideas on aesthetic *conflict* and the use of the models that were constructed by Meltzer using concepts that emerged from the experience of the transferential relationship. I will come back to the notion of the aesthetic model later on. Such a model could provide analysts with an appropriate link between what is observed in clinical practice and the theories implemented to undertake that practice.

It is no surprise that Meltzer (1984) called the Freudian model a *neurophysiological* or *hydrostatic model*, since Freud produced his body of work at the climax of modern science, at a time when classic thermodynamics of reversible and balanced processes were the scientific paradigm.

A couple of decades later, Melanie Klein designed a new model, in which the "geography" of fantasy, in terms of spaces in the mind and in objects, is centre stage. From 1934 onwards, with the splitting of the self and its objects, the "inner world" became a world of images which, as the theory was developed, were renamed "internal objects." Meltzer referred to this Kleinian theory as a *theological model*, as he proposed that people profess a sort of "religion" in which their internal objects play the role of "gods," who perform regulatory functions within the internal world.

In addition to Freud's neurophysiological model and Klein's theological model, Meltzer explored a third one, Bion's he described it as *epistemological*, given its connection to knowledge and thinking. Finally then, going back to the *aesthetic model*, it was Meltzer who brought the spotlight on the development of the mind: taking into account that psychoanalysis always provides a space for aesthetics, he introduced the notion of the *aesthetic conflict*.

Now, having traced Meltzer's journey through the different psychoanalytic models, the same could be done with the development of his ideas.

To outline a general summary of this development, it could be said that his ideas on the subject of the aesthetic conflict first emerged in the context of his work with autistic children, which resulted in the publication of his book *Explorations in Autism* (1975) and his further exploration and publication of the book *The Apprehension of Beauty* (1988). In the latter, Meltzer put forward that the essence of the aesthetic conflict is that the impact of beauty cannot exist without conflict, and that conflict lies between what can be perceived—the beautiful exterior—and the interior—which cannot be observed—which is unknown, mysterious and disturbing.

The aesthetic object is highly capable of stirring emotions: it is a conflictive combination of passion and anti-passion. But the mythical question is whether the interior of the object—as opposed to the exterior perceived by the senses—is as beautiful as the exterior. Mental development would occur if one were to tolerate this unanswered question, that is, if one were able to withstand the slow construction of the notion of essential mystery in other people's interior, which is nothing but the mystery of the world itself.

Therefore, given that autistic persons are not able to tolerate emotional turbulence, the aesthetic conflict leads them to disaggregate emotional experiences, and to become mentally detached. Meltzer asserts that autistic children express the tragic failure of the human spirit, the failure regarding the impossibility to understand beauty being unable to tolerate it being inaccessible and mysterious.

Coming back now to the starting point of this chapter—analytic practice and the role of the analyst—the consequences of the aesthetic model in our daily practice sessions are still to be unveiled.

The Meltzerian notion of *transference*, even if it remains deeply rooted in its Freudian origins as both a resistance to and an evocation of the past, resembles Klein's approach, which indicates that transference is not a re-actualization of the past but an externalization of the relationship with internal objects in the here and now of the analytic session.

From this point of view, the potential to develop a transferential relationship stems from the infantile parts of the self and is constantly present, but it is not always reachable by analytic work, as it is easily seized by the narcissistic organization which not only cannot identify the transference, but also to develop a transferential relationship.

In my opinion, the formulation of the aesthetic conflict introduces an approach according to which the aesthetic issue constitutes a founding category for a model of the mind, and thus changes from adjective to the noun "conflict."

The possible aesthetic model entails a specific concept of truth made up of three components:

a   The idea formulated by Bion about truth as the necessary food for the mind to grow;
b   The idea—already aesthetic in and of itself—that truth is mysterious, that it is an impending revelation.

Linking these two ideas, it could be argued that the vicissitudes of mental life and of possible development takes place in the realm of one's ability to live in and maintain the mystery triggered by the encounter with an opaque, non-transparent object.

c   The idea that the love for truth is related to the capacity to appreciate the beauty of the object. This is the concept of truth raised by Meltzer, who quotes Keats in stating that beauty and truth are one and the same (1988).

Considering these three points, beauty then involves a contact with the inaccessibility of the aesthetic object. As such, the aesthetic paradigm would be that truth *is beauty, insofar as the existence of the inapprehensible mystery can be tolerated and there is the capacity to withstand it.*

The analytic relationship is a new type of relationship in which a person—the analyst—is available for understanding but on the basis of accepting his/her own limitations in terms of knowledge. In turn, what is transferred by the patient becomes an object that can be intuited and conjectured, though its interior cannot be grasped by the senses.

In a talk Meltzer delivered in Buenos Aires in 1990 (1990), he said that transference is not a fact, but more of a construction in the mind of the analyst and that, in devising an interpretation, the analyst gives an opinion to the patient that may shed light on something happening in the patient's mind and, therefore, may help them to continue thinking.

Therefore, since I am referring to the act of suggesting opinions on what happens in transferential relationships, it is not possible to speak of *correct interpretations*; in fact, analysts who work with this approach in mind become much more dependent on the monitoring of their countertransference. This way of thinking about the transference, brings us closer to exercising the possibility of tolerating doubt, not knowing and uncertainty; something more along the lines of a "negative capacity," as Bion puts it.

I believe that this point is crucial, and even more so in the work we do with children and adolescents: analysts should strip themselves of any expectation, any goal they may have other than helping to continue to develop and alleviating the suffering of their patients.

I mention all of this as it is useful to remind ourselves that, in today's world, we need to remain alert in distinguishing between *aims* and *aspirations*. In doing so, we will be able to sincerely acknowledge whether or not we are falling in the trap of responding to the goals expected for our patients—particularly in the case of children and adolescents—by their families, educational institutions or any other agent likely to put pressure on them.

Now, to continue exploring the effects of the Meltzerian model on our practice, I am going to focus on psychoanalytic interpretation. While this is not the only way one intervenes in a session, it is still a fundamental tool in our daily work.

I have been interested in this subject for a long time. My enthusiasm converged with an invitation I received to give the key note speech at the

IPA Congress in Boston in 2015 (2015). There I referred to the analyst's toolbox and focused on psychoanalytic interpretation: I presented clinical material from a case of a five-year-old boy. The material I presented was over 30 years after I had worked with him. Moreover, I pointed to the changes I had noticed in my way of working and I discussed the changing times at large, for example, the advancement of technology, the emergence of different sexualities and new modes of parenting, among others.

However, while there is no doubt that these factors have had a great impact on the processes of subjectivation, is also true that Meltzer strongly pointed out the need to take into account the context in which the processes of subjectification takes place. He always saw psychoanalysis as closer to art than to science; considered its transmission as a process far removed from a pedagogical perspective. He maintained that the possibility of a person's development was closely linked to having an object in the external world capable of awakening an aesthetic reciprocity.

With regards to the processes of subjectivation, classical philosophy has considered, from its conception, that the subject always presents itself as coagulated. In its classical sense, the word "subject" implies a certain *unity*.

In psychoanalysis, Freud challenged the hegemony of consciousness by postulating the subject of the unconscious, which does not follow the lineaments of formal logic.

At present, it is known that subjectivities are not solely comprised of the subject of reason, as classical and modern philosophy suggested, nor only of the subject of the unconscious. The contemporary conception of subject entails an interaction with time and an environment. Moreover, the process of subjectivation is never-ending: instead of people remaining fixed characters, new versions of subjectivity are constantly being produced.

Furthermore, the role of the human other in the constitution of the subject is no longer disputed—this process can only occur as an intersubjective construction.

Meltzer (1988), in proposing the notion of aesthetic conflict, takes Klein's proposal a step further by establishing that a baby's first engagement with their mother's breast—as a representation of the beauty of the world—positions them, from the outset, in a conflict between what can be perceived, that is, the beautiful exterior, and the interior, which is non-observable, mysterious, only conjecturable, which becomes a tormenting source of anxiety. With his formulation of the aesthetic conflict as a mythical moment of the beginning of mental life, Meltzer postulates that the recognition of otherness takes place right from the start and that the ability to accept this radical difference is present all through a lifetime. This statement introduces a radical change from Kleinian theory by postulating that the depressive position could precede the paranoid-schizoid position, perhaps as a fleeting, foundational moment of contact with an object of great beauty that cannot always be tolerated.

Going back to the notion of psychoanalytic interpretation. In psychoanalytic discussions, we often talk about creation and the contents of analysts' interpretations, however, it is also interesting to study the context in which interpretations are formulated. If both aspects are taken into account, it becomes evident that Meltzer's model has had an important impact on them in relation to analytic practice.

Let us begin with the genesis—the creation of the content. In relation to the Kleinian theological model, there is a prevalence of hostility at the outset of life, when the death drive is perceived and later on deflected out of a fear of annihilation. Papers that presented clinical examples over 40 years ago illustrate a way of interpreting—certainly different from Melanie Klein's—that was centred on presence of hostility in the transference, which narrowed the understanding of what was happening in the analytic field, moreover, it was not helpful in dealing with patients' paranoid anxieties.

This does not mean I am denying the existence of negative transference. On the contrary, I consider its interpretation to be essential, but it should always be in counterpoint to the recognition of libidinal impulses, which are what ultimately allows patients to be in our sessions talking and playing with us.

This exclusive Kleinian perspective might have been the reason for the exacerbated number of interpretations as well as for the lack of tolerance of silence. All these factors might have led analysts to often formulate interpretations out of their own defensive movement and not because patients needed them.

As for the formulation of the interpretations, the aesthetic model and Meltzer's insistence on the practice of observation—especially of babies— according to the method devised by Esther Bick, we may speak of a *change in the modality of interpretation*, based on the possibility of observing and describing. In several texts, Meltzer points to the *descriptive* focus, instead of the *explanatory* focus, of formulation. This approach seems to me one that combines observation, reflection and conjecture.

This way of thinking about interpretation is consistent with the aesthetic approach, since patients are mainly offered descriptions. In addition to their content, these interventions *meta-communicate* an observational attitude, a skill that is somewhat estranged from the patient. It is an invitation to observe mental states. Therefore, this approach incites analysts to formulate interpretations from a humbler point of view, though not in terms of moral humbleness. If that were the case, reluctance would emerge from the aesthetic model itself, given the radical impossibility to fathom the essential mystery of the other. There is no transparency—there is opacity resulting naturally in a diffident attitude taken to arrive at possible early formulations of an interpretation, which can be expressed in phrases such as, "It seems to me…" or "I think that…"

The language of analysis is more different to the language of science—which cannot express everything, yet does not give up on trying to—than to the language of the arts, which acknowledges the impossibility of expressing everything.

In this line of ideas, in *Studies in Extended Metapsychology* (1986), Meltzer quoted Wittgenstein: "What cannot be said must be shown." However, in the context of the focus of the present contribution, this statement could be rephrased as follows: What cannot be said should be silenced and shall become a field to be shown. What is shown represents the ineffable boundary, and in my opinion, that is what is *meta-communicated* through the analytic attitude; it is not about what must not be said, but about that which *cannot* be said because of the limitations of language.

When I use the term "meta-communication," I am alluding to Bateson's work (1979), who said that the relation between the message and the topic is neither simple nor direct. If the receiver wants to try to understand something that is transmitted by the speaker, they must assimilate the encoding of the sender's message. Messages of this type, which are neither about the sender nor the receiver, but rather have to do with the code itself, are called *meta-messages*.

It is a difficult task to illustrate such a subtle and potentially evocative notion when it comes to each particular analyst's practice, as they are singular and follow their own style. For that reason, I am offering below a brief clinical illustration that was included in the paper I presented in 2000 in Firenze at the conference celebrating Meltzer, attended by the master himself (2000).

In her fourth year of analysis, and soon after starting her Monday session, a young patient said to me—in a very moving and inquiring tone—that she had made up her mind to invite me to her university graduation ceremony, which was to take place in two months' time. Then she remained silent.

I didn't respond, nor felt the need to. A moment later, she went on talking about how difficult she had found it to come to this decision, but that she felt that my being there would mean a lot to her. She said that it would have never crossed her mind to invite me to a party, like her birthday party, but that this was different.

She kept quiet again and then said that she had been talking with her boyfriend, and that they thought that surely I would not want to go, because that would entail a breaching of the analytic setting. She went silent again, this time for longer, and said that after giving it some thought, perhaps I would not want to go because I might think that I would make her feel more anxious.

With this brief fragment of a session, I want to explore the different choices I might have made at different stages of my own career as an analyst.

I might have remained silent in keeping with the idea that analysts should not answer questions. I could have formulated an interpretation of the meaning of my presence at her graduation: a projection of her infantile self onto me when present at the primal scene. I could have chosen a different line of action, a possible acting out or provocation to reject her invitation, since my engagement with the analytic method as a "graduate" myself actually prevented me from taking part in her graduation ceremony. I could have replied, "Thank you for inviting me," in a more colloquial tone.

The fact is that I did not respond. I now believe that I used my countertransference as an indicator, since I did not feel any pressure or need to reply. I did not speak at that moment because I did not feel it was necessary to do so. I really did not know what to tell her. I think that I decided to take her question and think about it until I could offer her something so she could continue thinking about her wish to invite me.

The session, of course, continued. Near the end, a transference configuration evolved, as the patient showed infantile features in her fear of dependency and an introjective type, with a concrete need of the presence of the object in order to gain control over it. Not only was this evident in the content of her words about her wishing I would attend her graduation, but also in the inquiring tone she used, which did not concretely formulate her wish.

This clinical example could support what could be considered an aesthetic thesis: what cannot be communicated can be meta-communicated. What can be shown is displayed as a surface, under which the patient must dive and work through by making assumptions.

In interpretations that follow scientific guidelines, what is relevant is that which is communicated. Conversely, in interpretations that would be appropriate for the aesthetic model, what is essential is the interplay between what is communicated and what is meta-communicated—for example, its coherence, or the slight difference or likely mismatch between the two.

Another consequence of the aesthetic model

Apart from the way of considering interpretation in the aesthetic model, the aesthetic model also has an impact that must be addressed: the notion of intimacy in psychoanalysis.

At first glance, this would seem to be outside the realm of psychoanalysis. However, upon further thought, we notice that our psychoanalytic "upbringing" is shaped by this notion. I trained as an analyst in the British-Kleinian and post-Kleinian traditions, comprised of authors who spotlight the key role of the *primal scene* in the Oedipal plot. Freud (1918) accorded great relevance to this scene, for instance, in the case of the Wolf Man.

In Klein's theory, the impulse to invade the primal scene, to invade what could be described as the parents' intimacy, acquires pre-eminence.

The play technique allowed Klein to offer this sort of interpretations to her young patients, who worked with her, listened to her, reacted and produced more material. There is no better example of this process than the work she carried out with Richard, her 10-year-old patient (1961). By means of this case, she demonstrated that analytic work can be engaged with a patient that is greatly suffering and that it has the potential to help them regardless of where the treatment is taking place.

During Richard's treatment, patient and analyst were in a multipurpose room that served as temporary shelter for children who had been evacuated from their homes due to the war. While Klein and Richard were holding their sessions regularly in a small town in Scotland, London was being relentlessly bombed. How could the analyst create an intimate space to engage in psychoanalytic treatment? Were conviction and passion, were the basic ingredients to make this experience possible?

Later on, Donald Meltzer (1973) expanded the notion of primal scene and developed his theory of the *sexual states of mind*, based on the potential configurations of this scene. In his view, adult sexuality does not provide material for analysis; it is an area linked to each person's innermost unconscious realities. Furthermore, adult sexuality is grounded in a state of introjective dependence on the internal parental couple and on the abandonment of the use of intrusive projective identification: "Face the wall, my darling" (ibid. 1973: 87). As for infantile sexuality, it does write the "script" of the primal scene introduced by Meltzer, and it adds more characters to the plot. The entire cast is made up of the father, the mother, the son, the daughter and the "baby inside the mother."

Years went by before Meltzer reformulated his ideas on mental spaces, the primal scene, and symbolization processes based on his work with autistic children. At this point, intimate relations acquired great relevance, as he considered them the field where emotional experience may unfold and give rise to thought, that is, where it may pave the way for symbolization.

It is precisely this point that makes it possible for Meltzer to offer a different perspective on intimacy, one that is no longer centred on the passions linked to the exclusion from the Oedipal scene or to parents' intimacy. Instead, his is focused is on the individual's contact with the essential mystery of a different other, one with a disturbing interior that provokes a passionate, overwhelming response.

In conclusion, I must say that I could have explored other aspects of clinical practice on which Meltzer's thinking has had great impact. I chose the notion of psychoanalytic interpretation because it has been a matter of interest to me for a long time. It is also true that it is not easy to determine and describe the profound influence that a master like Meltzer, not only on the way we work in psychoanalysis, but also on the way we live our lives and how we observe and think about where the world we live in is headed.

Meltzer has conveyed to us the importance of observation in psychoanalysis and of the practice of Esther Bick's method of infant observation. Twenty-five years ago, Meltzer himself encouraged experienced analysts in Buenos Aires to form what could be called a "pilot" group, which was supervised by fax on a weekly basis with the invaluable help of the Tavistock Clinic in London.

Having that experience and learning of Bick's method thereafter enabled us to test and redefine the rule of abstinence by means of concrete experiences, which caused some turmoil in the way Bion conceptualized this notion of the term.

We were also able to grasp a fact that had also been formulated by Bion and creatively revamped by Meltzer: it is not possible for our sense organs to seize the qualities of the phenomena of our daily analytic work, and neither is it easy for us to describe them with our language. Therefore, we use the words we know to describe the facts of the so-called "psychic reality," which can be sensed in the transference-countertransference matrix and in people about whom we can only make assumptions and draw inferences, as I have done myself following the teachings of Meltzer.

In closing, I would like to state that, to keep within the bounds of the living tradition, one must engage in internal dialogue, respect for dream life and dream interpretation, and continuous practice this internal work on an almost daily basis.

All of the above can be summarized in two points: on the one hand, we experience great passion for a job that can hurt when it appeals to us; and on the other, that detailed observation of both the world and ourselves is at the very core of a task we are called to time and time again, like the poet's muse.

References

Bateson, G. (1979). *Mind and Nature: A Necessary Unity*. Hampton Press, 2002.

Freud, S. (1918). *From the History of an Infantile Neurosis*, S.E., Vol. XVII, 17: 1.

Klein, M. (1961). *A Narrative of Child Analysis. The Writings of Melanie Klein*, Vol. IV. London: The Hogarth Press, 1975.

Meltzer, D. (1967). *The Psycho-Analytical Process*. Pertshire: Clunie Press.

Meltzer, D. (1971). A. Hahn (ed.) Towards an atelier system. *Sincerity and Other Works*. Collected papers of Donald Meltzer. London: Karnac Books, 1994.

Meltzer, D. (1973). *Sexual States of Mind*. Clunie Press.

Meltzer, D. (1975). *Explorations in Autism*. London: Clunie Press.

Meltzer, D. (1984). *Dream Life: A Re-examination of Psychoanalytic Theory and Technique*. Pertshire: Clunie Press.

Meltzer, D. (1986). *Studies in Extended Metapsychology*. London: Clunie Press.

Meltzer, D. (1988). *The Apprehension of Beauty*. Pertshire: Clunie Press.

Meltzer, D. (1990). Conferencia. *Psicoanálisis, Journal of the APdeBA*, Vol. 15, No. 2, 1992.

Ungar, V. (2000). "Transference and aesthetic model," presented at the International Congress "The development of the psychoanalytic method. Theoretical and clinical studies of Donald Meltzer's contributions to psychoanalysis," Florence, Italy, February 2000. *Psicanalise, Journal of the SBP,* Vol. 2, No. 1, 2000.

Ungar, V. (2015). The toolbox of the analyst trade: Interpretation revisited. *International Journal of Psychoanalysis,* 96: 595–610.

Index

For Product Safety Concerns and Information please contact our EU
representative GPSR@taylorandfrancis.com
Taylor & Francis Verlag GmbH, Kaufingerstraße 24, 80331 München, Germany

www.ingramcontent.com/pod-product-compliance
Lightning Source LLC
Chambersburg PA
CBHW050613280326
41932CB00016B/3022

9 781032 579702